T0006175

NEW TESTAMENT
EVERYDAY BIBLE STUDIES

NEW TESTAMENT
EVERYDAY BIBLE STUDIES

REVELATION

WITNESS AND WORSHIP
IN THE WORLD

SCOT MCKNIGHT

QUESTIONS WRITTEN BY
BECKY CASTLE MILLER

HarperChristian
Resources

New Testament Everyday Bible Study Series: Revelation
© 2024 by Scot McKnight

Requests for information should be addressed to:
HarperChristian Resources, 3900 Sparks Dr. SE, Grand Rapids,
Michigan 49546

ISBN 978-0-310-12961-5 (softcover)
ISBN 978-0-310-12962-2 (ebook)

HarperChristian Resources titles may be purchased in bulk for church,
business, fundraising, or ministry use. For information, please e-mail
ResourceSpecialist@ChurchSource.com.

First Printing November 2023 / Printed in the United States of America

23 24 25 26 27 LBC 5 4 3 2 1

CONTENTS

For MANT 2018 and the Gertie Girls

GENERAL
INTRODUCTION

Christians make a claim for the Bible not made of any other book. Or, since the Bible is a library shelf of many authors, it's a claim we make of no other shelf of books. We claim that God worked in each of the authors as they were writing so that what was scratched on papyrus expressed what God wanted communicated to the people of God. Which makes the New Testament (NT) a book unlike any other book. Which is why Christians are reading the NT almost two thousand years later with great delight. These books have the power to instruct us and to rebuke us and to correct us and to train us to walk with God every day. We read these books because God speaks to us in them.

Developing a routine of reading the Bible with an open heart, a receptive mind, and a flexible will is the why of the *New Testament Everyday Bible Studies*. But not every day will be the same. Some days we pause and take it in and other days we stop and repent and lament and open ourselves to God's restoring graces. No one word suffices for what the Bible does to us. In fact, the Bible's view of the Bible can be found by reading Psalm 119, the longest chapter in the Bible with 176 verses! It is a meditation on eight terms for what the Bible is and what the Bible does to those who listen and read it. Its laws (*torah*) instruct us, its laws (*mishpat*) order us, its statutes direct us, its precepts inform us, its decrees guide us, its commands compel us, its words speak to us, and its promises comfort us, and it is no wonder that the author can sum all eight up as the "way" (119:3). Each of those terms still speaks to what happens when we open our minds to the Word of God.

Every day with the Bible then is new because our timeless and timely God communes with us in our daily lives in our world and in our time. Just as God spoke to Jesus in Galilee and Paul in Ephesus and John on Patmos. These various contexts help us hear God in our context so the *New Testament Everyday Bible Studies* will often delve into contexts. Most of us now have a Bible on our devices. We may well have several translations available to us everywhere we go every day. To hear those words, we are summoned by God to open the Bible, to attune our hearts to God, and to listen to what God says. My prayer is that these daily study guides will help each of us become daily Bible readers attentive to the mind of God.

REVELATION

INTRODUCTION: READING THE BOOK OF REVELATION

The best opening to this Book was written by Gordon Fee, so I quote him to get us started:

> Stepping into the Revelation from the rest of the New Testament is to enter into a strange, bizarre new world; and this is true even in the days of *The Lord of the Rings* and Harry Potter. Instead of narratives, arguments, or plain statements of fact, the Revelation is full of angels, trumpets, and earthquakes; of strange beasts, dragons, and bottomless pits. Most believers, therefore, take one of two extremes: some simply avoid it in despair; others take an exaggerated interest in it, thinking to find here all the keys to the end of the world.

His next sentence is exactly right: "Both of these positions . . . are simply wrong" (Fee, *Revelation*, ix). Fee describes the book well, takes a quick look at each of the poles of interpretation, and then knocks the poles down. Thus, a different approach is in order, for him, and for me in this Everyday

Bible Study series. I join Kathleen Norris, whose fine ear for what Revelation is all about led her to write:

> The literature of apocalypse is scary stuff, the kind of thing that can give religion a bad name, because people so often use it as a means of controlling others, instilling dread by invoking a boogeyman God. . . . It is not a detailed prediction of the future, or an invitation to withdraw from the concerns of this world. It is a wake-up call. . . . Maybe we're meant to use apocalyptic literature in the same way: not as an allowance to indulge in an other-worldly fixation but as an injunction to pay closer attention to the world around us. (Norris, *Amazing Grace*, 318, 319)

The Book of Revelation is an apocalypse, and for many generations it was called "The Apocalypse of St. John." An apocalypse opens a drawer or a file or a door or a window onto inside information. Divine inside information, something unveiling, or a revealing of who God is and what will happen on the earth at the hand of God. Soon.

You will need your imagination to understand this book. Ellen Davis said this perfectly:

> If it weren't for the book of Revelation's way of presenting the gospel, *The Lord of the Rings* never could have happened. Because St. John the Divine, like Tolkien long after him, knew that the best way to strengthen faith is to get Christians' imaginations fired up. He understood that God works through our imaginations to touch our hearts. So John gives us powerful verbal images—not empty fantasies but true symbols that guide us as we probe the world with our imagination.

> Isn't that why God gave us an imagination anyway, so
> we could look with the eyes of faith beyond surface
> impressions, and see what is really going on in our
> world? (Davis, *Preaching the Word*, 312)

Imagination for what God wants out of God's people in God's world, and one clear lesson in this book is that God has searching eyes on politics, on political corruption, and on corrupt political leaders. At any and all levels. Let's not pussyfoot around with this book and pretend it's not about politics. So, we will have some sidebars throughout this book that touch on sensitive political topics, like Christian nationalism and de-Christianized progressivism. One singular problem that ties political zealots on both sides of the aisle has been said in the recent memoir by Yahoo! News political correspondent Jon Ward, who wrote after growing up into adulthood in conservative evangelicalism, that those with a strong political agenda among conservative evangelicals "acted as if America and the kingdom of God were the same thing" (Ward, 107). I may be unpopular today to stand between our two political parties, pointing my fingers at both for the same sin, namely, thinking the kingdom and our nation are the same, but stand there I will. But I stand there (in this book and have for decades in my public speaking and writing) because I think both sides get some things right and some things wrong.

Before we open the Book of Revelation, the sins of Babylon in this book are timeless and therefore timely for us: idolatries, immoralities, and injustices. We'll get to that, but we will also get to three timeless visions of how followers of Jesus, the Lamb of God in Revelation, are to live when they are surrounded by these three timeless sins: wisdom to discern the presence of these sins, a solid witness to Jesus in words and life, and a worship that centers God and the Lamb so powerfully that believers are emboldened in their witness to be dissidents of the corrupted powers at work in today's many, varied Babylons.

FOR FURTHER READING

Ellen F. Davis, with Austin McIver Dennis, *Preaching the Luminous Word: Biblical Sermons and Homiletical Essays* (Grand Rapids: Wm. B. Eerdmans, 2016). [Davis, *Preaching the Word*] pp. 310–316.

Gordon D. Fee, *Revelation: A New Covenant Commentary* (Eugene, OR: Cascade Books, 2011).

The quotation from Kathleen Norris comes from her book, *Amazing Grace: A Vocabulary of Faith* (New York: Riverhead, 1998).

Jon Ward, *Testimony: Inside the Evangelical Movement that Failed a Generation* (Grand Rapids: Brazos, 2023).

WORKS CITED IN THE STUDY GUIDE

(Throughout the Guide you will find the author's name and title as noted in this book listing with page numbers whenever I cite something from it):

Brian K. Blount, *Revelation: A Commentary* (Louisville: Westminster John Knox, 2009). [Blount, *Revelation*]

Greg Carey, *Faithful and True: A Study Guide to the Book of Revelation* (Cleveland: Pilgrim, 2022). [Carey, *Faithful and True*]

Ellen F. Davis, with Austin McIver Dennis, *Preaching the Luminous Word: Biblical Sermons and Homiletical Essays* (Grand Rapids: Wm. B. Eerdmans, 2016). [Davis, *Preaching the Word*]

Gordon D. Fee, *Revelation: A New Covenant Commentary* (Eugene, OR: Cascade Books, 2011). [Fee, *Revelation*]

I will make extensive use of a book I wrote with Cody Matchett called *Revelation for the Rest of Us: A Prophetic Call to Follow Jesus as a Dissident Disciple* (Grand Rapids: Zondervan Reflective, 2023). I will refer to it as [McKnight-Matchett, *RRU*].

McKnight, Scot, *The Second Testament: A New Translation* (Downers Grove: IVP, 2023). [McKnight, *Second Testament*]

Ian Paul, *Revelation: An Introduction and Commentary* (Downers Grove: IVP Academic, 2018). [Paul, *Revelation*]

Jeffrey A.D. Weima, *The Sermons to the Seven Churches of Revelation: A Commentary and Guide* (Grand Rapids: BakerAcademic, 2021). [Weima, *Sermons*]

HOW TO BEGIN AN APOCALYPSE

Revelation 1:1–8

[1] *The revelation from Jesus Christ, which God gave him to show his servants what must soon take place. He made it known by sending his angel to his servant John,* [2] *who testifies to everything he saw—that is, the word of God and the testimony of Jesus Christ.* [3] *Blessed is the one who reads aloud the words of this prophecy, and blessed are those who hear it and take to heart what is written in it, because the time is near.*

[4] *John,*

To the seven churches in the province of Asia:

Grace and peace to you from him who is, and who was, and who is to come, and from the seven spirits before his throne,

[5] *and from Jesus Christ, who is the faithful witness, the first-born from the dead, and the ruler of the kings of the earth.*

To him who loves us and has freed us from our sins by his blood,

[6] *and has made us to be a kingdom and priests to serve his God and Father—to him be glory and power for ever and ever! Amen.*

> ⁷ *"Look, he is coming with the clouds,"*
> *and "every eye will see him,*
> *even those who pierced him";*
> *and all peoples on earth "will mourn*
> *because of him."*
> *So shall it be! Amen.*

⁸ *"I am the Alpha and the Omega," says the Lord God, "who is, and who was, and who is to come, the Almighty."*

I've never written a dystopian novel or an apocalypse. If I did, I'd do what John did, or at least I'd try. John kick-starts the letter by telling us what the entire book will be about. His opening contains just three words (in Greek): "apocalypse [of] Jesus Christ" (my translation). What about that word "of"? Was it an apocalypse *from* Jesus as in the NIV? Or an apocalypse *about* Jesus Christ? Yes and yes, and yet, John was not so specific. Because "from" and "about" are true to the whole book, I prefer "The Yēsous Christos apocalypse" (McKnight, *The Second Testament*). That little word "of" in brackets a few lines back is not as clear as either "from" or "about," and that's how this apocalypse, this revelation, begins, with a *Jesus-Christ kind of unveiling*. An opening three-worder that leads us straight to Jesus, who becomes the center of attention in the next passage (1:9–20).

Because the listeners to this Book heard the word apocalypse first, they probably weren't surprised when John said, "because the time is near" (1:3). Theologians call this "eschatology," the doctrine of last or ultimate things. The entire Book of Revelation works into our heads and hearts to give us an eschatological framework for understanding our world. Kathleen Norris was born into such a worldview. She tells us in her wonderful book *Amazing Grace* that the "model of the Norris family Crest that my father found in England reads 'Regard the End.' Maybe eschatology is in my blood" (Norris, 12). John would want the same crest for his family.

Several terms jump up for attention in today's passage.

WITNESSING

Notice what happens here. There's a staircase of witnesses from the Throne of God all the way down to Patmos and from Patmos a mail service of some sort to each of the seven churches. Brian Blount describes 1:1–3 as a "chain of witness" (Blount, *Revelation*, 27). "God," John tells us, "gave" this apocalypse to "him" (Jesus Christ) "to show to his slaves" [NIV has "servants"], one of whom was John. But, between Jesus and the slaves is the "angel" of the Apocalypse who came to John (1:1). Reception of this Apocalypse makes John himself a witness (NIV has "who testifies" in 1:2) to the "word of God" and to the "Jesus-Christ-witness." John "saw" both what was spoken and written as the word of God and the Jesus-Christ-witness (NIV: "the testimony of Jesus Christ"). Put into a mathematical expression: the apocalypse = God's word = Jesus-Christ-witness.

John opens then by informing his readers, actually hearers, that what he sent to them to be read to them comes from God. Big claim. That's what apocalypses do.

BLESSING

I just corrected myself in mid-sentence by saying "readers, actually hearers" because of what John writes in 1:3. John "saw," and what he saw he wrote down, and what he wrote down was given to someone who read it to others. John writes "Blessed is the one who *reads aloud* the words of this prophecy, and blessed are those *who hear it* and *take to heart* what is written in it, because the time is near."

Someone was given the assignment, a person called a *lector* (a professional reader), to read this entire book aloud to seven different churches in western Asia Minor. Aloud. Can you imagine doing that yourself? I have never read the whole book aloud in one sitting in my life. When the lector read the book, people asked questions, which the lector answered. And some people frowned, and the lector would have perhaps asked, "Why are you frowning?" And others showed faces of confusion, so the lector would have ad-libbed to make it clearer. Reading this book would have been a long afternoon or a long evening, or both—with something to eat while it was being read.

The listeners are blessed too because they get to hear the God-sent and mediated Apocalypse. But the deepest blessing goes to the one who both listens or hears it and observes it or keeps it or does what it calls people to do. We will look at the three themes of Christian practice in this book later, but I can tell you now they are (1) wisdom for discernment, (2) witness, and (3) worship. The blessing comes to those who read it and listen to it and then live it out in at least those three ways.

READING

Verse four sounds like this is a letter, but it's not strictly a letter. Most think it is a combination of three types of written communication: an apocalypse, which it is according to 1:1; a letter, which appears to be the case in 1:4 and 2:1–3:22; and a prophecy, which it is in 1:3 and 22:18. So, yes, it's all three even though we will suggest at 2:1 that those "letters" may not quite fit the genre of a letter and are, instead, messages. Ian Paul wonders if John's shift in types of literature might create "interpretive vertigo" in us (Paul, *Revelation*, 64)!

Because the term "prophecy" gets confused by many, I offer an analysis of what a prophet is: A prophet is someone who (1) gets a message from God, (2) speaks that message from God to the people of God, and the prophet's calling (3) is to offer a divine diagnosis of the condition of the people of God and (4) issues the requirement to repent, and then the prophet predicts that, (5) if the people repent, blessing comes, and (6) if they don't repent, judgment comes.

Revelation is front to back prophetic. Prediction is only one part of a prophet's message, and often not even the most important. To call Revelation a prophecy then is not to suggest it is filled with predictions of specific events. A prophet who chooses to wrap a prophetic message in the language of the apocalyptic turns the book away from a pile of predictions and toward a message for the seven churches. In the broad sweep of this book, John will declare what will happen to the opponents of God, wrapped up in "Babylon" in Revelation 17–19, for the sake of the seven churches so they will be strengthened in their witness and worship of Jesus Christ as the world's true ruler.

The Apocalypse is sent to "the seven churches in the province of Asia." John informs that God—through Jesus, through the angel, through John—sends them "grace and peace." God is here called "the one who is, and who was, and who is to come" (1:4; cf. 1:8; 4:8; 11:17; 16:5). That grace is from God but also from the "seven spirits before his throne," which is John's language for the Holy Spirit (cf. 3:1; 4:5; 5:6). And that grace comes also from Jesus, who is the "faithful witness" himself in both speaking and living, but he is also the one who was first raised of those who will be raised, and he is also "the ruler of the kings of the earth" (1:5). The size of those congregations in Asia Minor was not large but John opens the Apocalypse with nothing less than an extravagant claim: this Jesus to whom they witness and whom they worship is the world's true king. Wow. Rome's response to that claim is to exile the author to Patmos (1:9). But please don't associate Patmos with a penal colony. The island, with its stunning views of the Aegean Sea, was populated and thriving. If he wasn't so devoted to pastoring those churches, one could wonder if John had not found himself a good spot for a sabbatical to write this most prophetic of books. Ian Paul says this eloquently, and so sets up the entire Revelation:

> In each of these, John draws on and adapts Old Testament terms and ideas, and expresses them in a way which presents a direct challenge to the dominant narratives in his day, starting the process of raising the stakes for his audience as they consider everyday questions of life and loyalty as a small minority in a vast and powerful empire. (Paul, *Revelation*, 58)

PRAISING

John turns immediately to worship and praise of Jesus in 1:5b–7. Jesus "loves us" always because already he "has freed us from our sins by his blood" and has actually—no one knew this at the time—"made us to be a kingdom and priests to serve his God and Father"—let's give God glory.

To open the Apocalypse, John announces, first, that Jesus is coming back to earth and the witness and worship of the believers are to keep their eyes on that return of Jesus; second, that everyone on planet earth will see Jesus when he returns; third, those who see him includes even those who killed him, who are every bit a part of the Rome that put John on Patmos; and fourth, the whole world will regret their part in putting Jesus to death and opposing the people who follow Jesus (1:7). Very apocalyptic. Very subversive, too. These are the beliefs of dissident disciples.

John steps back and utters a word he just heard from God's own lips: "I am the Alpha and Omega, who is, and who was, and who is to come, the Almighty" (1:8). These words will be said as well by Jesus (21:6; 22:13). John could not have had a higher view of Jesus than equating him with God the Father.

QUESTIONS FOR REFLECTION AND APPLICATION

1. How does it impact your understanding of Revelation to know it was read aloud to the seven churches?

2. What three types of written communication are used in Revelation?

3. Consider John's use of the Old Testament. Look at Zechariah 4:2–6 and compare John's "seven spirits." See Psalm 89:37 as a source for "faithful witness" and Psalm 89:27 as a source for "kings of the earth." Consider Exodus 19:6 for "kingdom and priests" and Zechariah 12:10 for "every eye will see him." What do these allusions or echoes say to you about John?

4. How have you heard Revelation taught in the past?

5. What do you anticipate learning in this study?

FOR FURTHER READING

Kathleen Norris, *Amazing Grace: A Vocabulary of Faith* (New York: Riverhead, 1998).

REVELATION BEGINS WITH JESUS

Revelation 1:9–20

⁹ I, John, your brother and companion in the suffering and kingdom and patient endurance that are ours in Jesus, was on the island of Patmos because of the word of God and the testimony of Jesus. ¹⁰ On the Lord's Day I was in the Spirit, and I heard behind me a loud voice like a trumpet, ¹¹ which said: "Write on a scroll what you see and send it to the seven churches: to Ephesus, Smyrna, Pergamum, Thyatira, Sardis, Philadelphia and Laodicea."

¹² I turned around to see the voice that was speaking to me. And when I turned I saw seven golden lampstands, ¹³ and among the lampstands was someone like a son of man, dressed in a robe reaching down to his feet and with a golden sash around his chest. ¹⁴ The hair on his head was white like wool, as white as snow, and his eyes were like blazing fire. ¹⁵ His feet were like bronze glowing in a furnace, and his voice was like the sound of rushing waters. ¹⁶ In his right hand he held seven stars, and coming out of his mouth was a sharp, double-edged sword. His face was like the sun shining in all its brilliance.

¹⁷ When I saw him, I fell at his feet as though dead. Then he placed his right hand on me and said: "Do not be afraid. I am the First and the Last. ¹⁸ I am the Living One; I was dead, and now look, I am alive for ever and ever! And I hold the keys of death and Hades.

¹⁹ "Write, therefore, what you have seen, what is now and what will take place later. ²⁰ The mystery of the seven stars that you saw in my right hand and of the seven golden lampstands is this: The seven stars are the angels of the seven churches, and the seven lampstands are the seven churches.

The Apocalypse doesn't jump immediately to visions of what is to come or start predicting events and people and the end of the world. Instead, the book begins by revealing Jesus Christ in a host of images and terms. Who Jesus is shapes what will be seen and heard by John. John's message for the church, about Babylon/Rome, and about New Jerusalem, begins by revealing who Jesus is. Before you pick where a house will be built on a land lot, you need to know who the architect is and how that architect works. It matters if it is a Frank Lloyd Wright home. I remember preparing to play golf one time in the Boston area with a veteran PGA tour player. When I asked him where we were going to play, he said something like this: "On a Donald Ross course in Concord." That meant nothing to me, but to my friend, "Donald Ross" told the whole story. He explained what that meant as we journeyed through a difficult (for me) golf course.

As we journey through the Apocalypse, we too will discover just how important today's passage, the beginning of Revelation, is throughout the book. The beginning is one word, one name, one person: Jesus.

Witness to Jesus

John informs his readers that he had been exiled to Patmos because of his "testimony of Jesus." This expression works the way the first three words of 1:1 worked: it could be a testimony *by* Jesus or a testimony by John *about* Jesus. Yes, of course, both fit. So a safe translation that sounds just like John's own words is the "Jesus witness" (1:9). Opposition to the growing Jesus-is-Lord movement did not become official persecution until later in the second century. A recent study about persecution in the history of the church by Wolfram Kinzig makes two important points, and I add numbers to the quotation to make the points easier to find:

> [1] Almost certainly there was no law or statute penalizing Christianity up until the reign of Trajan (98–117). [2] Imperial officials, therefore, acted solely by virtue of their power of coercion (*coercitio*), allowing them to deploy any policing measures required to maintain public order, including the death penalty. (Kinzig, *Christian Persecution*, 31)

So, John's exile to Patmos was more locally rooted in the authorities in Ephesus than issued out of the offices of Domitian in Rome.

On the "Lord's Day," a day dedicated to Jesus the Lord, John was "in the Spirit," which puts him on the same shelf as the prophets, and in the Spirit he heard a "loud voice like a trumpet" (1:10). John is now explaining the chain of witnesses we read about in 1:1–3. John tells his readers that, "When I saw him, I fell at his feet as though dead"

(1:17; sounds like Daniel 10:7–10), revealing that he had nothing less than an ecstatic, overwhelming experience. And he lived to tell us! More importantly, he lived to "write" about what he heard and saw (1:11, 19). He wrote because Jesus commanded him to. John's Revelation then is his witness, his testimony, his verbalized experience of Jesus and what the angels sent from Jesus wanted him to see, hear, and know.

VISION OF JESUS

In the harbor of the island of Rhodes, which is not far from Patmos, was the Colossus, a massive, 100-foot statue of Helios, the sun god.* What everyone—visitor or native—saw was a memorial to a military victory of the third century BCE. By the time John was prophesying in western Asia Minor, the Colossus of Rhodes no longer stood, having collapsed in an earthquake. But the story was known. It was one of the seven wonders of the ancient world. In the "harbor," that is, chapter one, of John's Apocalypse is nothing less than a Colossus of Jesus.

My New Testament has some twenty-five cross references to the Old Testament for these verses and these many references show once again how immersed John is in Scripture. Consistent with how he borrows from his scriptures throughout the book, so in the seven letters that follow, John borrows something about Jesus for each of the churches. This Colossus of Jesus that we meet in chapter one has his eyes on each of the churches, and what he sees is not always good, which is also why John wrote this book.

---

* The Colossus Christ idea was first sketched in *Revelation for the Rest of Us* (pp. 169-170) and I have borrowed most of that section in what follows.

The Jesus of the Apocalypse is revealed in today's passage, and one of the best ways to grasp what is said requires slowly reading the passage and marking every little detail about Jesus. Here are the ones I have marked and, as you read these, ask yourself where else in the Bible you meet such descriptions of heaven-sent messengers. Notice, too, that the images and terms collide with one another and roll out like a box of toys tossed upside down.

A day is dedicated to Jesus (1:10).

He orders John to write (1:11).

John somehow "saw" the "voice" and he sees "seven golden lampstands" (1:12).

He was "like a son of man," wearing a "robe" down to his feet with a "golden sash around his chest" (1:13).

His hair was "white like wool, as white as snow" and his eyes were "like blazing fire" (1:14).

His feet were "like bronze glowing in a furnace" and his voice, shifting from the sound of a trumpet, like "the sound of rushing waters" (1:15).

His right hand gripped "seven stars" and very noticeably a "sharp, double-edged sword" proceeded out of his mouth (1:16).

Let's be honest: if you slowed down to read this passage and visualized it with your imagination, well, you saw a gruesome figure. Greg Carey rightly says, "this portrait has defied those artists who have attempted straightforward representation" (Carey, *Faithful and True*, 18). Yet, an overwhelming and lordly and profoundly encouraging Jesus for John. He couldn't wait to start writing. What John saw is nothing less than a mosaic of Old Testament images and figures, especially what is found in Exodus about the high priest, and in Daniel 7's and Daniel 10's wonderful figures of the Son of Man and angels. If you'd like to focus on one passage, much of the vision here comes from Daniel 7:9–18. Ian Paul sums it up well:

> Part of this picture is of Jesus as High Priest, the one who mediates for us before God, and this idea is reinforced by the absence of anyone resembling a priest in the visions of worship and Revelation 4–5. Second, much of his appearance makes him resemble the Ancient of Days, God himself on his throne; he is the "image of the invisible God" (Col. 1:15) and the "exact representation of his being" (Heb. 1:3). Third, he resembles an angel, a messenger from God, the one who communicates to us through his life words and actions the revelation of God that we need to hear. Fourth, he displaces all counterfeits that we might find in other religions; it is he, and no other, who nourishes us and holds the keys to the most vital questions of life and death. While human empires rise and fall, his Kingdom is everlasting for it is trustworthy and true. It is his words which cut through to the truth, confirming what is right and refuting what is false. The light of his countenance offers us the light of life. (Paul, *Revelation*, 75)

That term "mosaic" says it all. But how much of it did John actually perceive? It seems he needed what comes next (vv. 17–20) in order to find the right words for the vision of Jesus he saw. Think of it this way: John could not write vv. 12–16 until Jesus gave him the words now in vv. 17–20.

INTERPRETATION BY JESUS

Jesus orders John not to fear because of who he is. That
he is the kind of Jesus he and the churches need, and to
return to the opening words in today's passage, John wants
them to know he is the "brother and companion in the
suffering and kingdom and patient endurance that are"
theirs "in Jesus" (1:9). He's with them as they hear this
book read aloud. More important, Jesus is with them. We
now get titles to add to the descriptions above, titles that
point us to figures. Jesus is the "First and Last" (1:17), the
"Living One" who was dead but was raised. And, too, the
one with the "keys of death and Hades" in his hand (1:18).
So the trumpet-blower dressed up in dazzling apparel is
none other than Jesus. He is about to reveal to John "what
you have seen, what is now and what will take place later"
(1:19).

Then a clear interpretation causes us to turn to John's
second chapter. Jesus apocalypses to John that the seven
stars are the "angels of the seven churches" and the seven
lampstands are the seven churches themselves (1:20). The
word "angels" translates a Greek word, *angelos*, that means
messenger, and it could be a messenger in or for that local
church who could read and explain this Apocalypse to
them, or it could be a divine-sent angel for each of those
churches. Which makes one wonder if every church
formed has an angel assigned to it. The answer is maybe,
but we can't be certain, so let's not speculate too much.
And the seven lampstands: is this a menorah or are these
seven separate lampstands?

We end with this: the vision John describes in today's
passage overwhelmed John. However, John was told by
Jesus that such a vision was not a cause of fear. It is a pity

that so many have learned to manipulate audiences, often younger audiences, to be scared out of their wits by this book. Jesus makes it clear that the panoply of visions in this Apocalypse are not to cause fear but witness and worship. We would do well to listen and learn and live it out.

We can find hope in the Apocalypse because it begins with a vision of a mighty resonant Jesus. With him, we can proceed forward with hope and encouragement. But before we can proceed forward, we need to leapfrog to Revelation 17's description of Babylon, for it is in that chapter that we encounter the *problem John was facing, not just in the public sector with Rome, but in the churches themselves.* Babylon "creep" was a distinct problem: the ways of Babylon were on the rise among the believers of western Asia Minor. John brings such Babylon creep up in Revelation 2–3 many times, but because we all have learned to wait to read chapter seventeen until we get there, we easily fail to see that the problem of Babylon was also a problem in the seven churches. So, we turn now to Revelation 17 so we can read Revelation 2–3 more accurately.

QUESTIONS FOR REFLECTION AND APPLICATION

1. How does Revelation itself serve as a witness and a testimony to Jesus?

2. How does understanding the history of official empire-wide persecution impact your view of John's exile?

3. What details do you notice about Jesus in this opening section?

4. What do you learn about Jesus in this section that helps you see "the kind of Jesus you need"?

5. What do you think it would take for people to change their view of Revelation from a book of fear and confusion into a book of witness and worship?

FOR FURTHER READING

Wolfram Kinzig, *Christian Persecution in Antiquity* (Waco, TX: Baylor University Press, 2021).

DISCERNING THE PRESENT

Revelation 17:1–18

¹ One of the seven angels who had the seven bowls came and said to me, "Come, I will show you the punishment of the great prostitute, who sits by many waters. ² With her the kings of the earth committed adultery, and the inhabitants of the earth were intoxicated with the wine of her adulteries."

³ Then the angel carried me away in the Spirit into a wilderness. There I saw a woman sitting on a scarlet beast that was covered with blasphemous names and had seven heads and ten horns. ⁴ The woman was dressed in purple and scarlet, and was glittering with gold, precious stones and pearls. She held a golden cup in her hand, filled with abominable things and the filth of her adulteries. ⁵ The name written on her forehead was a mystery:

BABYLON THE GREAT
THE MOTHER OF PROSTITUTES
AND OF THE ABOMINATIONS OF THE EARTH.

⁶ I saw that the woman was drunk with the blood of God's holy people, the blood of those who bore testimony to Jesus.

When I saw her, I was greatly astonished. [7] *Then the angel said to me: "Why are you astonished? I will explain to you the mystery of the woman and of the beast she rides, which has the seven heads and ten horns.* [8] *The beast, which you saw, once was, now is not, and yet will come up out of the Abyss and go to its destruction. The inhabitants of the earth whose names have not been written in the book of life from the creation of the world will be astonished when they see the beast, because it once was, now is not, and yet will come.*

[9] *"This calls for a mind with wisdom. The seven heads are seven hills on which the woman sits.* [10] *They are also seven kings. Five have fallen, one is, the other has not yet come; but when he does come, he must remain for only a little while.* [11] *The beast who once was, and now is not, is an eighth king. He belongs to the seven and is going to his destruction.*

[12] *"The ten horns you saw are ten kings who have not yet received a kingdom, but who for one hour will receive authority as kings along with the beast.* [13] *They have one purpose and will give their power and authority to the beast.* [14] *They will wage war against the Lamb, but the Lamb will triumph over them because he is Lord of lords and King of kings—and with him will be his called, chosen and faithful followers."*

[15] *Then the angel said to me, "The waters you saw, where the prostitute sits, are peoples, multitudes, nations and languages.* [16] *The beast and the ten horns you saw will hate the prostitute. They will bring her to ruin and leave her naked; they will eat her flesh and burn her with fire.* [17] *For God has put it into their hearts to accomplish his purpose by agreeing to hand over to the beast their royal authority, until God's words are fulfilled.* [18] *The woman you saw is the great city that rules over the kings of the earth."*

Note to the Reader: We insert our reflection on Revelation 17 here so we can be ready to read Revelation 2–3, and in doing so we set up the vision of John for disciples. He's calling followers of the Lamb to be dissidents against the way of the dragon and Babylon.

Each book of the New Testament requires a special sensitivity. Each was written for a specific audience at a specific time. The present timeless message emerges from its original timely relevance. The problem for the seven churches of western Asia Minor, the original audience of Revelation, was Rome. John makes a profound choice when he decides in chapter seventeen to label Rome with the name "Babylon." By giving Rome the name "Babylon," John informs his readers and listeners that Rome needs to be seen as no different than the ancient, corrupt, tyrannous city of Babylon. By the way, calling Rome "Babylon" was a popular thing to do in John's day. Other apocalyptic writings call Rome Babylon, and another author in the New Testament, Peter, does as well (1 Peter 5:13). John makes it abundantly clear that he's talking about Rome because he decodes the word "Babylon" for us when he says it was the city of seven hills and the world's "great city that rules over the kings of the earth" (Revelation 17:9, 18).

The problem for John is Babylon. Babylon shows up in the public sector of opposition to the gospel, persecution of the churches, and pressure on believers to conform to the ways of Rome, *and also* Babylon makes its presence felt in the messages to the seven churches.

THE CHOICE OF
ANCIENT BABYLON

The people of the Bible, Israel, oriented their memory around two tragedies in their history: captivity in Egypt and exile in Babylon. So trenchant was that memory that Isaiah has two chapters of a "prophecy against Babylon" (Isaiah 13–14), and Jeremiah, who mentions the city over and over, weighs in with two long chapters in another prophecy against Babylon (50–51). Both Ezekiel and Daniel carry on these words of prophetic judgment against the city. Babylon became for Jews and then for early, especially Jewish, Christians a graphic image that stirred the memory of a tyrannous city full of ego, injustices, and oppression of the people of God. When you had had your fill of a city and its powers and its injustices, you called it "Babylon."

Babylon was for John as timely as it was timeless for his contemporaries. When John sorts out Babylon's corruptions in chapters seventeen, eighteen, and nineteen, he is not thinking of some future city twenty-one centuries later (Moscow, for instance). Babylon, for him, evokes the timely message of his own day. As John sat in exile from his churches on the island of Patmos, Babylon evoked Rome. And nothing other than Rome. The timeliness of Babylon was used by one contemporary Jewish writer both for Rome and for Asia. You can read these two uses in a book called *4 Ezra* (3:1–2; 15:46–47, see J. Charlesworth, gen. ed., *Old Testament Pseudepigrapha*, Vol. 1:516–559).

To catch what John is doing in calling Rome Babylon, we might ponder which other cities and powers the oppressed people of the world have seen in similar categories. Most don't call such a city "Babylon," but they do use the city's name with tension in the heart and disgust on the tongue: London for colonial Americans, Berlin for Jews of the 1930s and 40s, Cape Town for twentieth century victims of apartheid, Chicago for coal miners in southern Illinois, and Washington, D.C. for persons of color experiencing systemic racism in the USA. You've heard the sneering pronunciations of such places as I have as well. When hearing such verbal suffering, we hear an echo of "Babylon" for the followers of Jesus in the seven churches.

THE MARKS OF JOHN'S BABYLON

After the introduction in chapter seventeen (17:1–2), John describes the vision he had (17:3–6a), which he did not understand and said so with the words, "I was greatly astonished" at the woman of his vision (17:6b). The angel sent to give him this vision understands his perplexity, so the angel turns to a full-on explanation of each element of the vision of the woman (17:6b-18). The explanations, and we do not need to cover each of them, combine with the vision to *provide us nothing less than marks of Babylon*. These marks are timely for Rome in John's day, but, because the insights are so timeless, the marks of Babylon become windows onto corruption in the powers of tyrants and empires and cities in our world. Once you see John's marks of Babylon you cannot un-see them. Hence, John provides for you and me categories to discern Babylon today. One of John's top values is wisdom that enables discernment.

The graphic image details a "great prostitute" who sits upon "many waters." She has engaged her acts of prostitution with the "kings of the earth" and offered her drunken bouts with the "inhabitants of the earth" (17:1–2). As we will see a number of times in Revelation, prostitution is idolatry, which may include sexual indulgence or not. The wines point us to the excesses of pleasure and immoralities. We should be careful not to restrict the behaviors to sex as what follows clarifies what the acts are.

First, the woman sits atop a "scarlet beast that was covered with blasphemous names" (17:3). Here we encounter idolatry, the sort on display everywhere in the ancient Mediterranean. Idols, gods, shrines, statues, monuments, flowers, offerings, sacrifices, and ceremonies for entire cities. The believers in the seven churches faced such blasphemous idolatries every day. Revelation is about politics because it is about religion, and since it is about religion, it is about idolatry, and since it is about idolatry, it is about politics.

The religious practices of these cities were not disciplines of a personal spirituality but a toxic mixture in which a person gained standing by expressing their allegiance to Rome. Religion was politics; politics was religion. Our requirement is to discern Babylon in our day so I will probe a theme or two here.

Christian nationalism reveals that same toxic mixture where flag and cross, nation and faith, are so combined that one does not feel comfortable in the groups unless one is willing to drape a flag round one's shoulders to express one's Christian faith. Two experts on Christian nationalism, Andrew Whitehead and Samuel Perry, offer this complex description:

> . . . a cultural framework—a collection of myths, traditions, symbols, narratives, and value systems—that idealizes and advocates a fusion of Christianity with American civic life . . . the "Christianity" of Christian nationalism represents something more than religion. As we will show, it includes assumptions of nativism, white supremacy, patriarchy, and heteronormativity, along with divine sanction for authoritarian control and militarism. It is as ethnic and political as it is religious. (*Taking America Back for God*, 10)

In Christian nationalism, religion is politics and politics is religion. When the two are combined, one has a pseudo-Christianity. One has idolatry. One is then in Babylon. Partisanship, whether it means to the Republicans or the Democrats, when it involves demonizing the other party and refusing to respect fellow citizens with the freedom of choice is a mark, not of one's faith, but of Babylon.

The antithesis of political idolatry is worship of the Lamb, and we will look at this theme in the pages that follow. For now, I want only to say that the more we worship the Lamb, the more we will discern Babylon, and the more we camp out in worshiping in New Jerusalem, the more we will see Babylon's corruptions. The political strife of Christians today owes its problems to the lack of genuine worship on the part of American Christians. (More in the rest of this book.)

Second, the woman of Revelation 17 is "dressed in purple and scarlet," the colors of pomp and royalty, and she was "glittering with gold, precious stones and pearls" and she "held a golden cup" (17:4). Words for this description include opulence, extravagance, affluence, lavishness, and prosperity. Mind you, all at the expense of others. By the time Revelation is written we move through the Roman emperors of Julius Caesar, Augustus, Tiberius, Caligula, Claudius, and Nero, as well as the year of four emperors (Galba, Otho, Vitellius, Vespasian), and then we have Titus and Domitian, who I think is the emperor at the time Revelation was written. All taxes that flowed to Rome flowed to the emperor, and all government benefits were from the emperor. What John describes here is nothing less than the madness of opulence by exploitation and theft by the emperors.

Third, the woman is a murderer, both by assassinations and by the military's death machine. The "woman was drunk with the blood of God's holy people, the blood of those who bore testimony to Jesus" (17:6). Here's how power worked in that world, which would be known to all Jews because of Herod the Great: most emperors, governors, and client-kings in alliance with Rome dealt with opposition by assassination. The Christian claim that Jesus was the world's true king was enough to kill people like Antipas, a Christian martyr (2:13).

Fourth, the woman runs a military machine that sucks the conquered into total allegiance to the woman. Notice these verses: "They have one purpose and will give their power and authority to the beast" and "For God has put it into their hearts to accomplish his purpose by agreeing to hand over to the beast their royal authority" (17:17). These are but minor indicators, but they are enough: Rome's emperor got the name "emperor" because he was a military commander who needed to be as successful on the battlefield as a conqueror of other armies (*imperator*).

Rulers of other countries either surrender to the emperor or they are murdered by the empire's death machine. At the heart of the woman's power, then, is intimidating, relentless military power.

Fifth, I will skip ahead to chapter eighteen to fill in the marks of Babylon. The woman was not only opulent, but she was an economic exploiter of the resources and human bodies of other nations. In chapter eighteen we read "and the merchants of the earth grew rich from her excessive luxuries" (18:3). A full display of the cargo in the endless stream of boats pointed toward Rome can be found in 18:11–13, which ends with "and human beings sold as slaves." Rome transported bodies to the Forum for sale the way colonial America transported African slaves to its own shores. That was Babylon, and the treacheries of Babylon are still with us, especially in our major cities.

Sixth, the pomposities of the woman we looked at above come to expression in chapter eighteen's expression of hubris and arrogance:

> In her heart she boasts,
> "I sit enthroned as queen.
> I am not a widow;
> I will never mourn." (18:7)

John got this one way back in Isaiah 47:7–8, where we read this:

> You said, "I am forever—
> the eternal queen!"
> But you did not consider these things
> or reflect on what might happen.

Now then, listen, you lover of pleasure,
    lounging in your security
and saying to yourself,
    "I am, and there is none
    besides me.
I will never be a widow
    or suffer the loss of children."

On walls in many major cities in the Roman empire was a lengthy list of accomplishments by the emperor Augustus. The arrogance of self-adulation is only matched by the narcissism of other political leaders and presidents whose accomplishments were less, but whose egos matched that of Augustus. Where you see arrogance, in a city or in a village or in a business or in a church, you are standing face-to-face with Babylon.

Not in the descriptions of Babylon in Revelation, but nonetheless behind what he writes, was the mark of **branding**. One could not walk two hundred yards in the center of Ephesus without encountering images reminding the Ephesians of the power of Rome. Images like idols, shrines, leaders dressed in the Roman way, the Latin language, and the ever-present powers of architecture embodying the impress of Rome on their city. Nothing wrong with production and manufacturing, but one cannot deny that at times "Made in America" can have the cachet of a proud producer and the sashay of triumphalism.

Babylon Today: Militant Secularism

I'm not of the view that evangelical Christians are persecuted in the USA, but I am of the view that secularism has made the Christian faith more and more difficult to affirm. What concerns me here, however, is *militant* secularism. What are the marks of this Babylon-ish mark in our world? Remember, a major mark of Babylon was its idolatry. That is, it did not worship the true God but false gods. Militant secularism, while bowing down to the non-transcendent idols of money, luxury, desire, and power, is both like and unlike ancient Rome. But the Apocalypse gives us wisdom to discern militant secularism as a manifestation of Babylon.

First, secularism stands at the opposite end of the combination of church and state in what is sometimes called Constantinianism. Constantine was the first Roman emperor to embrace the Christian faith and then, to one degree or another, imposed faith on the empire. Most civilized societies have not been secular because most combined culture, society, government, and religion. The Roman empire's many religions were woven into its politics and public life.

Second, modern secularism levels the playing field so all can play with freedom and equality. Social and theological tolerance and support of one another marks good secularity. Secularism prevents one religion from taking over a country.

Secularism, according to some, is a good thing—it is America living its Constitution in tolerating persons and ideas that differ from one another.

Third, secular*ization* describes the growth of secularism in order to enhance toleration and freedom.

But, fourth, *militant* secularism refers to the "gradual decrease in religious observance by the deliberate marginalization of religion from state institutions and the public square. The difference [between secularism and militant secularism] is whether one prizes freedom of religion or freedom from religion."

Fifth, militant secularism works for religion to become entirely private and socially invisible. Religion, thus, is seen as toxic for a flourishing society.

Sixth, the goal of radical forms of militant secularism is totalitarian conformity, requires intolerance of religion, and in the USA means the intolerance of anything smacking especially of traditional Christianity.

Seventh, as Mike Bird concludes his sketch of the rise of militant secularism, "Instead of a benign brand of secularism with a place for religion over here and the common spaces over there, now we are being fed a narrative that says religion is part of the problem, a toxic power that threatens the fabric of our civilization, a menace to equality and justice, and religion is the one thing preventing our society from being tolerant, diverse, peaceful, and inclusive" (Bird, *Religious Freedom*, 10, 42).

Wisdom

One gets no joy in describing the woman Babylon nor in pointing out the corruptions of our own country. But Revelation not only invites us to acquire wisdom to discern Babylon creep in John's day, but it requires us to perceive the threats of Babylon in our own world. John calls us to see it and to say it. To see it and refuse to acknowledge it leads us into compromise and capitulation to the way of Babylon in our world. This list of seven marks will not cover everything, but it's a start. Ours is not to copycat John but to discern Babylon in our world. Ours is to become, like John and those who heeded his words, dissidents of Babylon while living in Babylon. Ellen Davis takes us where this book wants us to go when she writes, "I think there is good evidence that Saint John was doing something more important and more urgent than encoding information on the end of the world for Christians 2,000 or more years in the future. He was writing to keep the church alive in his own troubled time. John was writing as a pastor, determined to reinvigorate the faith of his people, when everything in the surrounding culture was aiming to kill it. Does this sound familiar to you?" (Davis, *Preaching the Word*, 311).

It's your turn now. John can guide you.

QUESTIONS FOR REFLECTION AND APPLICATION

1. What was the context of the problem facing the seven churches?

2. What is McKnight's argument that Revelation is about politics? Why do you agree or disagree?

3. How does worshipping the Lamb serve as an antidote to political idolatry?

4. In what ways does exploitation serve as a mark of Babylon? Where do you see exploitation in the world today, and how does it help you identify Babylon?

5. What would you identify as the biggest problem facing your church today? What might John write about to warn you today?

FOR FURTHER READING

Michael Bird, *Religious Freedom in a Secular Age: A Christian Case for Liberty, Equality, and Secular Government* (Grand Rapids: Zondervan Reflective, 2022), 3–47, quoting p. 10, 42.

The Fourth Book of Ezra in J. Charlesworth, gen. ed., *The Old Testament Pseudepigrapha*, 2 vols. (New York: Doubleday, 1983). Translation of *4 Ezra* by B.M. Metzger, volume 1.516–559.

Andrew Whitehead, Samuel Perry, *Taking America Back for God: Christian Nationalism in the United States* (Oxford: Oxford University Press, 2020).

On Reading Revelation 2–3

Revelation 2–3 contains what has been called "letters" to the seven churches. Experts on ancient letters, however, agree that these are not technically letters. Instead, they can be called "messages" sent to each of these churches.

The problems showing up in the seven churches, and only two are exempted from the diagnosis of problems by Jesus, are the result of Babylon creep, or the impact of the ways of Rome on the faith and practices of believers in these churches. Disciples of Jesus are called to be double dissidents: they resist the way of Babylon, and they resist the way of Babylon creeping into the churches.

The promises to the seven churches correspond to the blessings and endless joys of New Jerusalem. Thus, the seven messages echo what will be found in Revelation 17–22. This helps our reading of the seven churches.

Each message can be organized in the following five categories: (1) Colossus Christ, (2) commendation, (3) Babylon creep, (4) correction, and (5) consequences, whether good (New Jerusalem) or bad (Babylon).

As for healthy vs. unhealthy churches, the messages are not optimistic: only two churches score as healthy (Smyrna, Philadelphia).

In the history of reading Revelation, some have claimed the seven churches correspond to seven periods of church history. Thus, each message becomes a prophecy of a period marked by the traits of that message. No church historian thinks these correspond well with periods in church history, and few believe this today.

A map of this region reveals that the book was sent to these churches in a circular path: starting in Ephesus going north to Smyrna and Pergamum, then turning south to Thyatira, Sardis, Philadelphia, and Laodicea (Weima, *Sermons*).

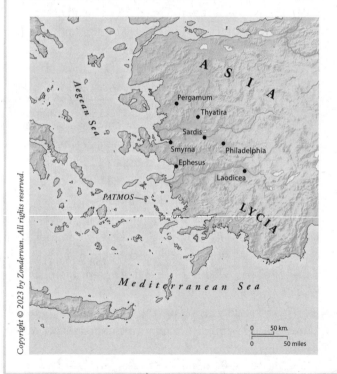

AN ORTHODOX
CHURCH
LACKING LOVE

Revelation 2:1–7

[1] *"To the angel of the church in Ephesus write:*

These are the words of him who holds the seven stars in his right hand and walks among the seven golden lampstands. [2] *I know your deeds, your hard work and your perseverance. I know that you cannot tolerate wicked people, that you have tested those who claim to be apostles but are not, and have found them false.* [3] *You have persevered and have endured hardships for my name, and have not grown weary.*

[4] *Yet I hold this against you: You have forsaken the love you had at first.* [5] *Consider how far you have fallen! Repent and do the things you did at first. If you do not repent, I will come to you and remove your lampstand from its place.* [6] *But you have this in your favor: You hate the practices of the Nicolaitans, which I also hate.*

[7] *Whoever has ears, let them hear what the Spirit says to the churches. To the one who is victorious, I will give the right to eat from the tree of life, which is in the paradise of God.*

I was there when Peter Scholtes' song, "They'll Know We Are Christians by Our Love," permeated evangelical churches in the late '60s and early '70s. Our high school youth group, I can say without exaggeration, could belt this song out when we got going. Which we did nearly every week for a year or more. I was also there when the 2010s got underway with unmasking the hypocrisies of Christian leaders and churches in how they have unlovingly treated people of color, women, and LGBTQ+ people. If the '60s and '70s helped the church's witness, the 2010s definitely wounded the church's witness.

Just like Ephesus. And just like Ephesus, we will need to reflect on this passage to see if and where we have lost our first love. And then listen to the wisdom of Jesus on what we can do to restore that love.

COLOSSUS CHRIST AND HIS COMMENDATION

Jesus, the Colossus in the "harbor" of Revelation, speaks to the church in Ephesus as the one who "holds the seven stars in his right hand" and as the one who "walks among the seven golden lampstands" (2:1). Jesus presents himself as the sovereign power over the guardian angels of each church, and Jesus is the one always present among all the churches. He's here, he's there, and he's watching.

By the time John sent this message to Ephesus, the city had experienced two major, and a variety of not-as-major, influences in the early church: the apostle Paul, the apostle John, and perhaps Mary the mother of Jesus, along with Priscilla, Aquila, and Apollos. On top of that, the church went through some difficult times with false teachers according to the Pastoral Epistles; the church was the setting for John's Gospel and three letters; and today's passage mentions Nicolaitans at work in Ephesus. The church had experienced challenges to accommodate itself to the ways of Rome, and the church had at times experienced the presence of wealthy Christians. The church had organized church leadership positions, and they were at the forefront of sorting out the ministry of women (for this paragraph, I rely on Paul Trebilco, *The Early Christians in Ephesus from Paul to Ignatius*).

With that history, Jesus has much good to say about the church in Ephesus (2:2–3). The church at Ephesus, which surely by then was more than one house church, was marked by good works (NIV has "deeds"), their labor (NIV: "hard work"), and their "perseverance." The NIV's choice of perseverance for some readers will suggest a Reformation understanding of genuine believers persevering. But John has the notion of resilience in mind. Furthermore, the more perseverance takes on its major theological sense, the less reason for the complaint and correction that follows.

And the Ephesians have resisted "wicked people," that is, people connected to the church who are corrupted in character and teachings. In several decades of itinerants stopping in to speak and remaining overnight at Ephesus, some came in as "apostles," and the Ephesians wisely evaluated and discerned their character. Jesus again affirms their resilience in that "they carried the load because of my name and have not become labored" (McKnight, *The Second Testament*). Overall, the church at Ephesus remained brilliantly orthodox to the gospel and early Christian theology. Jesus will again emphasize their orthodox faithfulness, with different words, in 2:6 in that they have resisted the Nicolaitans. These commendations seem so strong one is surprised by the depth of Jesus' complaint that follows.

Orthodoxy without love kills because lacking love deconstructs whatever one believes.

Babylon Today: Civil Religion(s)

Civil religion wears many outfits.

First, for some, civil religion stands in the middle between a militant, radical secularism that wants either a total separation between church and state or the erasure of religion from the public square— and a radical religious nationalism in which the state and religion are fused. In this kind of tolerant civil religion, the church and the state overlap in ways that permit the church to be the church and the state be the state.

Philip Gorski, a historian of the church-state relationship and a strong proponent of this middle ground kind of civil religion, says "the basic formula for civil religion in American history has been prophetic religion [the Old Testament prophets' vision for justice and peace] plus civic republicanism, or, more succinctly, prophetic republicanism." Gorski thinks the vision for this historic vision of civil religion is diversity, not disbelief (Gorski, *American Covenant*, 19).

Some would contend such a public civil religion will wear down the witness of those who follow Jesus and thus see civil religion as a kind of secularism.

Second, Michael Gorman defines civil religion with an eye on Babylon and empire making their way into our context. So he defines it in the following terms:

> The attribution of sacred status to secular power (normally the state and/or its head) as the source of divine blessing, requiring devotion and allegiance of heart, mind, and body to the sacred-secular power and its values, all expressed in various narratives, other texts, rituals, and media that reinforce both the secular powers sacred status and the beneficiaries' sacred duty of devotion and allegiance, even to the point of death. (Gorman, *Reading Revelation*, 46–47)

Michael Bird, an Australian Bible scholar, thinks a fusion of church and state is at work in "civil religion," and he connects civil religion to Christian nationalism. He sees civil religion as a "syncretistic fusion between Christianity and nationalism" and "an increasingly close fusion of religion, nationalism, and ethnicity. This can express itself in the form of xenophobia toward immigrants and refugees, claims that only leader X is going to protect our religious and civil liberties against the socialist barbarians at the gate, or even a kind of God-is-on-our-side mentality that can be used to justify all sorts of crimes."

Bird continues: "but America is not a new Israel

> or the kingdom of Christ in advanced form. American Christians are not a bit closer to the throne of God. God does not have a covenant with America. America at its best is a paragon of democracy and a beacon of freedom to the nations of the world. America at its worst, with its racial injustices, insatiable greed, and military violence, is just another expression of Babylon the Great!" (Bird, *Religious Freedom*, 80).

BABYLON CREEP AND CORRECTION

The complaint is both simple and penetrating: "You have forsaken the love you had at first" (2:4). The traditional author of Revelation is the apostle John, and he was known eventually as the apostle of love for two reasons. First, his amazing chapter thirteen in his Gospel is where we got the "They'll Know We Are Christians by Our Love" lyrics, and 1 John which somehow manages to get the word "love" in seemingly most verses in the entire letter. Love for John begins with a God who *is* love, with God loving humans, with God sending his Son for our redemption, with humans responding to God's love by loving God back, and with humans loving one another. John has a theology of love that is nothing less than a cycle of love generating love. Somehow, and we don't know for sure, that cycle has been broken like a bad link.

What caused the breaking of this link of love? We can surmise that at least in part the pressure of local authorities in Ephesus turned these believers more inward, and stiff-armed them from being able to form into the kind of fellowship of love they previously had. Perhaps fear of persecution set in, perhaps stress over economic hardships had formed in their hearts, and perhaps the pressure to participate in public acts of allegiance to Rome had de-throned the lordship of Christ. We can't be sure of the details, but we do know the problem John discerned in the churches was Babylon "creep" that was reshaping how the believers lived.

So Jesus offers three steps of correction: (1) to remem-ber how far they have fallen (NIV's "consider" could be sharpened with "remember"), (2) to turn around, to con-vert back, and (3) to "do the first works" they had done in an earlier phase of their Christian faith (2:5). We would be wise not to turn this into some kind of trusty formula for regaining one's passions and affections in Christ. Yet, the cognitive and the behavioral are combined here in a way that makes sense to many of us even today. Perhaps the Ephesians heard this being read aloud and immediately returned in their imaginations to their early days in the faith and remember what it was like—and then perhaps they returned to those ways.

CONSEQUENCES

Jesus spells out the consequences for these believers in Ephesus. If they fail to repent, he will "remove your lamp-stand." The image could at least suggest that the church will collapse from its role as one of the two or three major churches of the time (Rome, Ephesus, Antioch of Syria). It may also suggest the elimination of the Ephesian church altogether. No one knows for sure. What we do know is that this kind of language grabbed the attention of the believers. If they do remember, turn back, and do the first practices, they will be "victorious" and get to nibble on the fruits of the tree of life in New Jerusalem, the "paradise of God" (cf. 2:7 and 22:2, 14, 19).

Unhealthy churches are exposed by Jesus to his scrutiny, but unhealthy churches are offered the opportunity to repent and return, which leads to victory and blessings.

QUESTIONS FOR REFLECTION AND APPLICATION

1. What commendations does Jesus offer the church in Ephesus through John?

2. How does Jesus, through John, criticize the church in Ephesus?

3. What course corrections are the Ephesian Christians told to make?

4. How would you evaluate your love for Jesus?

5. What would you like the Holy Spirit to do in your heart to help you be more loving?

FOR FURTHER READING

Michael Bird, *Religious Freedom in a Secular Age: A Christian Case for Liberty, Equality, and Secular Government* (Grand Rapids: Zondervan Reflective, 2022), quoting pp. 80, 82.

Michael Gorman, *Reading Revelation Responsibly*, (Eugene, OR: Cascade Books, 2011), 46–47, all in italics in original.

Philip Gorski, *American Covenant: A History of Civil Religion from the Puritans to the Present* (Princeton: Princeton University Press, 2019), quoting p. 19.

Paul Trebilco, *The Early Christians in Ephesus from Paul to Ignatius* (Grand Rapids: Wm. B. Eerdmans, 2007).

A CHURCH SUFFERING WELL

Revelation 2:8–11

8 *"To the angel of the church in Smyrna write:*

These are the words of him who is the First and the Last, who died and came to life again. 9 *I know your afflictions and your poverty—yet you are rich! I know about the slander of those who say they are Jews and are not, but are a synagogue of Satan.* 10 *Do not be afraid of what you are about to suffer. I tell you, the devil will put some of you in prison to test you, and you will suffer persecution for ten days. Be faithful, even to the point of death, and I will give you life as your victor's crown.*

11 *Whoever has ears, let them hear what the Spirit says to the churches. The one who is victorious will not be hurt at all by the second death.*

Jesus looks at the church in wealthy Smyrna, modern-day Izmir, and sees a healthy church. But you may be surprised what made this church healthy. It was not butts in the pew, bills in the plate, baptisms in the water, or buildings on the campus—the four measures many use today for success in a church. No. Not for Jesus. What made the church of Smyrna healthy was that it was suffering well.

That's right: the mark of this healthy church was suffering, and suffering the way Christ did. Their suffering was at the hands of local leaders in Smyrna (think Babylon) as well as at the hands of synagogue leaders distancing themselves from this radical, growing Jesus movement.

COLOSSUS CHRIST AND HIS COMMENDATION

The Colossus Christ commends the church in Smyrna as the "First and Last" and as the one "who died and came to life again" (2:8), both of which titles for Jesus were mentioned in the vision of Jesus in chapter one (1:17–18). The first cannot but have evoked the sense that Jesus was God (cf. Isaiah 41:4; 44:6; 48:12). Jesus comforts the Smyrnans because he has been there: he knows what it means to suffer, but he also knows the other side of suffering, namely, the power of the resurrection. What this means for the church is that their Lord is more powerful than the hands who make them suffer. History, like the stars of 2:1, is in his hands.

Along with his victory beyond death, the suffering of Jesus requires mention because the Smyrnans are experiencing "afflictions" and "poverty" and "slander" (2:9). The word "afflictions" is not your run-of-the-mill hassles, for often in the New Testament this word points at a cosmic-connected oppression, injustice, and tribulation against God and God's people. The Smyrnans experience the afflictions in three ways: as (1) economic hardship (cf. Hebrews 10:34) because of their witness and worship. Along with those came discomfort with the interplay of Babylon's paganism and social life, including the pressure to participate in the imperial cult; (2) as imprisonment, though only for a short while, and (3) as slanderous rumors or denunciations by tattlers among their Jewish opponents of the gospel (2:10). Just like Jesus, just like Stephen, just like Paul (cf. Mark 8:31–9:1; Acts 7:54–8:1; 2 Corinthians 11:16–32). The churches in Smyrna were no longer part of the synagogue, and the synagogue surely experienced social pressure from the authorities for those who had usurped the Jewish faith and morphed into Jesus faith. As Greg Carey puts it, "Any Christian who wanted to do business or advance in society would be confronted with" the various religions on offer (Carey, *Faithful and True*, 30). Smyrna, like Ephesus, was recognized by Rome as a "temple keeper" dedicated to Tiberius (cf. Acts 19:35). Jews were exempted from this religious practice, but it appears the Christians were not recognized as part of the synagogue and were in trouble with the authorities. What John calls the "synagogue of Satan" deserves more than wisdom today because it can easily slide in our culture into anti-Semitism.

EXHORTATION VS. CORRECTION

Jesus has no complaint against the church in Smyrna, but he does have an exhortation. And because there is no evidence of Babylon creep into this church, the word "correction" used in five of the seven messages seems misguided. I like the word "exhortation" instead, which has a double focus: "Do not be afraid" and "be faithful" (2:10). The two work together for those who suffer because fear can lead to denial of one's faith (think of Peter in Mark 14:66–72). So Jesus exhorts them to have courage and be allegiant or faithful to him by facing death knowing that the suffering will only be for "ten days" (Revelation 2:10), but the victory of life with God and resurrection comes on the other side.

CONSEQUENCES

Those who remain faithful, that is, who are double dissidents against the way of Babylon and its creeping presence in the church, will be given "life as [their] victor's crown" (2:10). Their crown may have been instead a wreath. That crown, however, is not material in the sense of something topped on one's head. Instead, their crown is life, eternal life, the second resurrection and not the "second death" (2:11; cf. 20:6, 14; 21:8). Their victory then is life in New Jerusalem.

QUESTIONS FOR REFLECTION AND APPLICATION

1. How is Jesus uniquely qualified to speak to the church in Smyrna about suffering well?

2. What type of afflictions were the Christians of Smyrna experiencing?

3. What exhortation does Jesus give them?

4. How do you think they received the message? How might it have landed for them?

5. What encouragement do you need today to help you be faithful and not fear?

A CHURCH WITH CORRUPTED THEOLOGY

Revelation 2:12–17

[12] *"To the angel of the church in Pergamum write:*

These are the words of him who has the sharp, double-edged sword. [13] *I know where you live—where Satan has his throne. Yet you remain true to my name. You did not renounce your faith in me, not even in the days of Antipas, my faithful witness, who was put to death in your city—where Satan lives.*

[14] *Nevertheless, I have a few things against you: There are some among you who hold to the teaching of Balaam, who taught Balak to entice the Israelites to sin so that they ate food sacrificed to idols and committed sexual immorality.* [15] *Likewise, you also have those who hold to the teaching of the Nicolaitans.* [16] *Repent therefore! Otherwise, I will soon come to you and will fight against them with the sword of my mouth.*

[17] *Whoever has ears, let them hear what the Spirit says to the churches. To the one who is victorious, I will give some of the hidden manna. I will also give that person a white stone with a new name written on it, known only to the one who receives it.*

Perhaps I'm unusual but it is hard for me to visit the various sites of churches in western Asia Minor and not have a thought go through my head. I'll explain. Not only is the presence of a church barely noticeable in this Muslim country, but the sites of these cities are mostly ruins. One cannot stand in the ancient sites of Pergamum or Ephesus or Sardis or Laodicea, which are indeed wonderful sites to visit, and not think about "what was and is no more." The warnings Jesus gives to these churches at times have haunted me when leading students around these sites. One can give a variety of explanations—like earthquakes and burgeoning cities in the flat plain below Pergamum—and they do bring me back to reality. But I never fail to experience the haunting warnings of these letters, not least the warning to Ephesus that Jesus will remove their lampstand (2:5).

One reason for the collapse of churches throughout the history of the church is when the teachings of the church wander from the gospel about Jesus into something catchier or political and modern and, well, you know the drill. Pergamum's problem was bad theology, and its bad theology exemplifies Babylon creep all over again. Bad theology is not just bad ideas; bad theology is a compromised discipleship. For the Apocalypse, this compromise means accommodating oneself too much to the ways of Rome, in which one's behavior reveals that one's theology is off base. American Christianity has far too many people captured by grasping for political power. The resemblance of this grasping and what was happening in the seven churches ought to be a loud trumpet blast of warning.

COLOSSUS CHRIST AND HIS COMMENDATION

One way to get people to listen to your ideas is first to affirm them publicly. It has a Latin name because one of the most famous orators of ancient Rome, Cicero, called it *captatio benevolentiae*, which means "capturing someone with good will." I get lots of emails from readers. When someone begins the letter with their version of a few lines of *captatio benevolentiae*, my eyebrows go up because almost always what follows is a criticism of something they disagree with in my writings. Fundraisers, evangelists, administrators, and leaders all do this—and the rhetorical technique of being nice before lowering the boom can be manipulative, and often is.

It can also be helpful and wise and pastorally warm. When done by the right person, in the right setting, to the right person. As when Jesus does it in these letters. The traits of Jesus in the message to Pergamum must have put the house churches in Pergamum on their heels: "These are the words of him who has the sharp, double-edged sword" (2:12; cf. 1:16; notice also Isaiah 49:2 and Revelation 19:15). Gulp. One of the Roman emperors' symbols was a sword or dagger, which means Jesus has removed the dagger from the emperor to enact divine justice. When Nero died and Galba became emperor, Suetonius tells us that Galba "began his march to Rome in a general's cloak with a dagger hanging from his neck in front of his breast" (Suetonius, *Galba*, 11). The sword used of Jesus here has a two-foot wooden handle with a double-edged, curved blade.

Such a sword, proceeding from the mouth of this Colossus Christ, judges and saves, deconstructs and reconstructs, ends injustice and forms justice. The sword-word of Jesus will not only act in the public sector against Babylon's injustices and idolatries, but in the church, the sword of Jesus prunes and pierces. Those who obey Jesus become dissidents of both Babylon and Babylon creep.

First, the pruning begins with recognizing what's healthy in Pergamum's Jesus movement (2:13). They are surrounded because they live "where Satan has his throne," which is both the Rome-anointed capital of Asia but also the seat of idolatrous worship and allegiance. Perhaps this "throne" refers to the massive, historic altar to Zeus on the acropolis of Pergamum, an altar now in a museum in Berlin. Perhaps, too, Satan's throne points to the healing center of Asclepius in Pergamum, and Asclepius typically had a serpent wrapped around his walking stick (Weima, *Sermons*, 97, has a picture of an Asclepius statue). Another: perhaps the throne refers to the imperial cult of Pergamum or to the pressure of persecution in the city. In that location they "remain true to [the] name [of Jesus]," that is, when they observed Antipas's murder for his allegiant witness to Jesus they "did not renounce" their allegiance to Jesus. One of the marks of Babylon was its murderousness, so much so that John says they were intoxicated on the blood of martyrs (17:6).

Babylon Today: Sexual abuse by church leaders

Thomas Fuller, *New York Times*, 12 August 2022

The leadership of the Southern Baptist Convention, the country's largest Protestant denomination, said on Friday that the church was under investigation by the Justice Department for sexual abuse and that it would "fully and completely cooperate."

Church leaders said in a statement that multiple branches of the denomination, which includes seminaries and missionary organizations, were under investigation and that the church was continuing to "grieve and lament past mistakes."

In May, leaders of the church published a scathing review that said reports of sexual abuse were suppressed by top church officials for two decades.

That investigation, which was conducted by an outside consultant, covered reports of abuse from women and children against male pastors, church employees and officials from 2000 to the present.

One of the report's most striking revelations was the existence of an internal list of 703 people suspected of abuse that had been compiled by an employee of the denomination's executive committee, its national leadership body.*

BABYLON CREEP AND CORRECTION

Their allegiance was not enough for Jesus because though they stuck it out in the midst of threats of death, their theology got mixed with "Balaam" and the "Nicolaitans"

---

* https://www.nytimes.com/2022/08/12/us/southern-baptist-convention-sexual-abuse.html.

(2:14–16). These terms evoke more than define, but the evocations appear to be about the mixture of the gospel with the ways of Babylon's idolatries. The worship of Baal mixed idol worship with sexual indulgences of all sorts (Numbers 25:1–5; 31:16), and this is the same kind of description used of the whore of Babylon in Revelation 17 (cf. 17:2, 3, 4, 13, 14; 18:2–3, 9; 19:3). So, I take the teachings of Balaam to be Babylon creep into the churches. Believers were participating too much in the public religious worship and in eating food offered to idols, which was at the same time an expression of allegiance to Rome. Balaam is a reasonably clear reference, but "Nicolaitans" is not. The same form of Babylon creep was mentioned about Ephesus as well (2:6), the difference being the Ephesians hated the teachings of the Nicolaitans. Perhaps this is the teaching of a man named Nicolaus; more likely it is a term for false teachings that combined idolatry, sexual misconduct, and allegiance to the emperor of Rome. Something similar will appear in his message to Thyatira (2:20).

Jesus' word of correction is "Repent!" (2:16).

CONSEQUENCES

If Pergamum's believers don't repent, Jesus will return to "fight against them with the sword of my mouth" (2:16). If they do and so become "victorious" in their allegiance to Jesus, Jesus will give to them both "some of the hidden manna" and "a white stone with a new name written on it" (2:17). Manna refers to God's special provisions (Exodus 16) and it became a promise for divine provisions in the final kingdom, with the word "hidden" referring to the jar of manna in the ark in the temple (16:32–34). The "new name," which sounds like Revelation 3:12 and 19:12, most likely points to a private name assigned by Jesus to each of his followers. The "white stone" probably refers to an admission ticket to New Jerusalem's banquet.

The ones who repent, who are victorious, are the ones like Antipas who was put to death. His trademark was that he was a "faithful witness" (2:13). The primary term used for the best way for believers to live in Babylon is to be a witness, and this term deserves now a brief explanation. The term belongs to a courtroom where someone was presented to a judge to witness or to testify about what they heard or saw. So the term becomes a "see" that is combined with a "say" that in Pergamum can lead to "suffering." A witness is someone who has *seen* something about Jesus that the witness knows is true, and that person has the courage to *say* what they believe to be true, knowing that the consequence of seeing and saying is that they could *suffer* for it. Brian Blount sums it perfectly when he writes "it is a word of provocative testimony and therefore active engagement, not sacrificial passivity" (Blount, *Revelation*, 29).

QUESTIONS FOR REFLECTION AND APPLICATION

1. When you reflect on the eventual destruction of the cities in these messages, how does that impact your understanding of the corrections and warnings?

2. How do Jesus' sword-words function when facing Babylon and the church?

3. What did the Christians of Pergamum do wrong in mixing their worship of the Lamb with worship of idols?

4. Consider McKnight's words, "bad theology is a compromised discipleship." How has bad theology impacted your discipleship journey?

5. What would it look like for you to grow as a witness for Jesus, who sees things about Jesus and says them, in spite of possible suffering?

A DIVIDED CHURCH

Revelation 2:18–29

¹⁸ "To the angel of the church in Thyatira write:

These are the words of the Son of God, whose eyes are like blazing fire and whose feet are like burnished bronze. ¹⁹ I know your deeds, your love and faith, your service and perseverance, and that you are now doing more than you did at first.

²⁰ Nevertheless, I have this against you: You tolerate that woman Jezebel, who calls herself a prophet. By her teaching she misleads my servants into sexual immorality and the eating of food sacrificed to idols. ²¹ I have given her time to repent of her immorality, but she is unwilling. ²² So I will cast her on a bed of suffering, and I will make those who commit adultery with her suffer intensely, unless they repent of her ways. ²³ I will strike her children dead. Then all the churches will know that I am he who searches hearts and minds, and I will repay each of you according to your deeds.

²⁴ Now I say to the rest of you in Thyatira, to you who do not hold to her teaching and have not learned Satan's so-called deep secrets, 'I will not impose any other burden on you, ²⁵ except to hold on to what you have until I come.'

²⁶ To the one who is victorious and does my will to the end, I will give authority over the nations—²⁷ that one 'will rule them with an iron scepter and will dash them to pieces like pottery'— just as I have received authority from my Father. ²⁸ I will also

give that one the morning star. [29] *Whoever has ears, let them hear what the Spirit says to the churches.*

One of the most stunning events I have learned about is what happened among the pastors and leaders in the post-World War II, post-Hitler churches. The question from everyone outside Germany was how complicit these pastors were in the tragedy called the "German Christians." German Christians, *Die deutsche Christen*, formed a Nazi Germany church that, to put it bluntly, de-Judaized the Bible and created a national church that was a profound disaster (*Nazi* shortens in German the word "national"). Some pastors and theologians spoke up; most didn't. Some who did, like Ernst Käsemann, Martin Niemoeller, and Dietrich Bonhoeffer, went to prison. Käsemann was in a prison camp; Niemoeller was Hitler's own prisoner; Bonhoeffer was murdered. Post WWII, German Christianity was profoundly divided *because of its compromise with the political powers* (see Hockenos, *A Church Divided*). They were dissidents of Babylon.

The church in Thyatira accommodated itself to the powers of Babylon in a way that, when taken to an extreme, led to the German Christian movement. A nationalized church not only accommodates itself to the powers but eviscerates the gospel and the church's capacity to speak truth to the powers. The USA's churches today are more like Thyatira than they may realize. Too many have capitulated to Babylon creep.

COLOSSUS CHRIST AND HIS COMMENDATION

The Colossus Christ who sends a message through John to Thyatira is "the Son of God, whose eyes are like blazing fire and whose feet are like burnished bronze" (2:18). As with the other titles for Jesus in these letters, we find the same expressions in the vision of chapter one (1:14, 15). Only in today's passage does "Son of God" appear in Revelation, but at least some would hear an echo of the title often used of Roman emperors, *divi filius* (son of a god). This Jesus challenges the imperial cult, merged as it was with the worship of Apollo Tyrimnos in Thyatira. The Son of God's eyes (Daniel 10:6) describe a penetrating perception of the conditions at Thyatira, and the "burnished bronze" feet may well describe a special metal made in the guilds of Thyatira (Weima, *Sermons*, 132).

The Son of God's commendations tumble out of a carton of virtues: good works, love, faithfulness, service, perseverance, and "now doing more than you did at first" (2:19). Their behaviors are in order, but Jesus knows there is a deep problem at work in Thyatira: they are divided. Some have fallen yet again for the compromised position of trying to follow the Lamb and Rome at the same time. One foot in Babylon and the other in New Jerusalem. First, Jesus turns to the accommodationists.

BABYLON CREEP AND CORRECTION

Jesus turns from labeling others with Balaam and Nicolaitans to "Jezebel," which became a trope in the Jewish world for an unfaithful woman. She was the Phoenician wife of the corrupted king Ahab, and she was known for murdering prophets (1 Kings 18–19). The label changes, but the sins are identical to the sins in Pergamum: that strange mixture of idolatry and sexual immorality (2:20). Jezebel fashions herself as a "prophet," which suggests to many that there is an actual woman in the church teaching these ideas. That the prophetess of Thyatira's name was Jezebel is unlikely. Babylon was surely creeping into the church.

One more time: the idolatries of western Asia Minor were more often than not tied to religious cults and public allegiance to the ways of Rome. Many scholars today think the Thyatiran idolatries and food practices connect the people to Thyatira's well-known and abundant trade guilds—unions of wool workers, bakers, etc.—that both sustained their income and provided feasts involving food offered to idols. Economics, religion, and politics were so mixed in that world that one could not have perceived a difference. Good citizens of these cities were public worshipers of the gods, and those who worshiped the gods expressed political support of the emperor. And when Christians mix faith with political religion, they compromise allegiance to Jesus. Either Jesus is Lord or Caesar is, Jesus is saying to Thyatira.

Yet, instead of a complaint, this divided church hears as well the commending words of Jesus to the faithful group: "the rest of you" here that have not been led to follow in the ways of Jezebel (=Babylon) and, speaking sarcastically, neither have they "learned Satan's so-called deep secrets" (2:24). So Jesus tells them he will not add any other burden than what was given in the Apostolic decree in Acts 15:28–29, which explains Jesus' concern with the idolatries and eating food offered to idols. So, he simply tells them to "hold on," or grip or grasp, "until I come" (2:25). Isn't it the truth that the problem people get all the attention in churches? I'd like to hear about the faithful holder-ons in Thyatira. What we can say for sure is that they are the ones whose virtues are given public affirmation in 2:19 above.

CONSEQUENCES

As one group gets complaint and another affirmation, so there are two consequences in the message of Jesus. The ones about whom Jesus is most concerned here are threatened with an awful judgment. The offer of repentance rejected, Jesus turns to graphic language of divine discipline of "suffering" and those who follow her ways will encounter the greatest of enemies, death itself. Their ends correspond to their "works" (NIV has "deeds"; 2:23).

The faithful group of dissidents will be "victorious" and will be handed "authority over the nations" and, along with that opportunity to rule in the New Jerusalem (which sounds like Psalm 2:9 and Matthew 19:28 and 1 Corinthians 6:2), they will also be given the "morning star," which could evoke Numbers 24:17, but the book of Revelation itself resolves this: the morning star is Jesus (Revelation 22:16). Again, the promise for the victorious is participation in New Jerusalem.

QUESTIONS FOR REFLECTION AND APPLICATION

1. What happens when churches capitulate to the Babylons of their day?

2. How does the church of Thyatira help illustrate the problems when behaviors seem right on the surface, but beliefs underneath are wrong?

3. How did the Thyatiran Christians make accommodation to public allegiance to Rome?

4. In what ways do you see economics, religion, and politics mixed in your world?

5. How do you struggle with "holding on" in your faith life?

FOR FURTHER READING

Matthew Hockenos, *A Church Divided: German Protestants Confront the Nazi Past* (Bloomington, IN: Indiana University Press, 2004).

THE ARROGANT CHURCH

Revelation 3:1–6

¹ *"To the angel of the church in Sardis write:*

*These are the words of him who holds the seven spirits of God and the seven stars. I know your deeds; you have a reputation [=**name**] of being alive, but you are dead.* ² *Wake up! Strengthen what remains and is about to die, for I have found your deeds unfinished in the sight of my God.* ³ *Remember, therefore, what you have received and heard; hold it fast, and repent. But if you do not wake up, I will come like a thief, and you will not know at what time I will come to you.*

⁴ *Yet you have a few people [=**name**] in Sardis who have not soiled their clothes. They will walk with me, dressed in white, for they are worthy.* ⁵ *The one who is victorious will, like them, be dressed in white. I will never blot out the **name** of that person from the book of life, but will acknowledge that **name** before my Father and his angels.* ⁶ *Whoever has ears, let them hear what the Spirit says to the churches.*

When does a church die? Or, better yet, why do churches die? Thom Rainer, a cataloguer of lists, has one on why churches die, and he lists: (1) because they refuse to admit they're sick, (2) they are waiting for the super pastor, (3) they don't take sufficient responsibility, (4) they are unwilling to change—at all, (5) they are too inwardly focused, and (6) they want to return to the glory days ("Why Are Churches Dying?"). When I Googled this question, there were numerous sites providing other lists. Numerous does not tell the story: 12.3 million results in 0.42 seconds! No two lists are the same. At one time a mainline expert claimed mainline churches were dying because they didn't have a robust enough theology or high enough expectations for Christians. Conservative church leaders loved that study, but they are now realizing their churches are dying, too! Another scholar said the decline of the mainline occurred because mainliners, rising up and up into the upper-middle and upper classes, were not having enough babies. Simple demographics. Other writers contend the secular age has made belief more and more difficult.

The church at Sardis, directly east of Smyrna and northeast of Ephesus, was dead. We will probe the symptoms of dying, thinking too that what Jesus urges for Sardis may speak to you and me about the health (or unhealth) of our churches. The problem at Sardis ties into a knot of naivete, arrogance, and laziness. Especially arrogance. Nothing evokes Babylon more than arrogance (17:5; 18:1, 7). Nothing warns a church of its demise and death more than arrogance. Arrogance presumes we are good enough, gifted enough, efficient enough, big enough, wealthy enough, successful enough, and busy enough to avoid disaster and to determine our desired results.

COLOSSUS CHRIST AND HIS COMMENDATION

The Colossus Christ who speaks a message to the church of Sardis is one who holds "the seven spirits of God" as well as the "seven stars" in his hand (3:1). Only in Revelation does the "seven spirits of God" occur (1:4; 4:5; 5:6), and those verses indicate they are before God's throne (1:4; 4:5). Yet, we read that the "Lamb had seven horns and seven eyes," and those seven eyes are "the seven spirits of God sent out into all the earth" (5:6). That the seven spirits appear between the Father and the Son in 1:4 makes it most likely that this is John's special language for the Spirit of God on mission. The Spirit brings life. Which means Sardis needs a fresh outpouring of the Holy Spirit.

Jesus finds precious little to commend about the church in Sardis. One could say they have some good works (NIV: "deeds") and a good "reputation" (3:1). Neither dresses any flesh on the bare bones of a dead body. But Jesus does come back to commendation in 3:4 when he observes that there are "a few people [the Greek has "names"] in Sardis who have not spoiled their clothes." And "not spoiled" is hardly a strong commendation. Jeff Weima concludes Jesus' words here do not add up to a commendation but are, instead, a concession (Weima, *Sermons*, 172). The metaphor of unsoiled clothing, in other words, temple-pure and white, most likely refers to moral uprightness, and perhaps also theological uprightness (6:11; 7:9, 13–14). Soiled clothing most naturally refers either to sexual sins (14:4) or to eating food offered to idols (1 Corinthians 8:7). Again, notice the two-fold expression of Babylon creep in the seven churches: idolatry and sexual immorality. All Jesus can muster is that some in Sardis have not fallen for idolatry and immorality. More than the "some" are the many who have compromised their allegiance to Jesus.

BABYLON CREEP AND CORRECTION

Jesus spots the reality that, though the church folk of Sardis think they are flourishing, they are dead (3:1). They lack self-awareness, like narcissists. Like Babylon. They assume their public image fools the crowds. Taking stock of their successes, they think they are on the side of the angels. But not Jesus, because he has "found [their] deeds unfinished in the sight of my God" (3:2). Those in Sardis connected to the church, like Ephesus, began well but have faltered and have become so lazy their mission work lies unfinished on the drawing room floor. They have failed to fulfill their discipleship. The theme of faltering shows up in 3:3 as well when Jesus reminds them what they "received and heard," namely the gospel about Jesus.

Five words express Jesus' correction for the church at Sardis. The first, "Wake up!" has often been said to evoke the sleepy, overconfident nature of Sardis as an impregnable city. Twice its exalted acropolis was captured by stealth—at night. The second, "Strengthen," assumes they have heard the gospel and begun walking the way of the Lamb but need more resolve to complete the tasks, while the third exhorts them to "Remember" the basics of the gospel (1 Corinthians 15:1–28) and gospel living that turns away from immorality and idolatry. Remembering is tied to the fourth, "hold it fast," while the fifth calls them to turn back ("repent") from their apathy (3:2–3). All five combine to form a full correction on offer for Sardis. They have succumbed to Babylon creep, and now they have to purge the place.

CONSEQUENCES

If they don't follow those corrections, Jesus will come "like a thief" to exercise divine judgment (3:3 and 16:15; cf. 2:5, 16, 25; 3:3, 11, 20). This warning reflects the words of Jesus (Matthew 24:42–43), Paul (1 Thessalonians 5:4), and Peter (2 Peter 3:10). Unlike the Sardis of old, they cannot rest secure in their presumed safety. No, they must "wake up" (3:3).

Those who have not fallen for the way of the dragon and Babylon "will walk with" Jesus dressed in the purity of "white" as those worthy of citizenship in New Jerusalem (3:4–5). Furthermore, their names will remain etched in the "book of life," never to be scratched out. The third expression of a good future for these believers is that the person's name will be openly recited—like a graduation ceremony—before "my Father and his angels" (3:5).

How many churches and church leaders have we watched in free fall and collapse in the last decade or two? Church experts may have found the technological problems and the strategic problems and the process problems, but at the core of church collapse is the arrogance to think it's all about us. Not just leaders but the entire culture of a church can drown itself in arrogance.

QUESTIONS FOR REFLECTION AND APPLICATION

1. What are some of the reasons you have heard for churches "dying"?

2. How has Babylon crept into the church of Sardis?

3. What is the significance of "names" in this section?

4. Examine yourself and your church. Where do you see arrogance creeping in that you want to be aware of?

5. Which of the three instructions to Sardis most resonates with you? "Wake up," "strengthen," or "remember"? Why?

FOR FURTHER READING

Thom Rainer, "Why Are Churches Dying?," accessed at https://churchleaders.com/outreach-missions/outreach-missions-articles/308041-dying-churches-die.html.

THE SMALL CHURCH

Revelation 3:7–13

⁷ *"To the angel of the church in Philadelphia write:*

These are the words of him who is holy and true, who holds the key of David. What he opens no one can shut, and what he shuts no one can open. ⁸ I know your deeds. See, I have placed before you an open door that no one can shut. I know that you have little strength, yet you have kept my word and have not denied my name. ⁹ I will make those who are of the synagogue of Satan, who claim to be Jews though they are not, but are liars—I will make them come and fall down at your feet and acknowledge that I have loved you. ¹⁰ Since you have kept my command to endure patiently, I will also keep you from the hour of trial that is going to come on the whole world to test the inhabitants of the earth.

¹¹ I am coming soon. Hold on to what you have, so that no one will take your crown. ¹² The one who is victorious I will make a pillar in the temple of my God. Never again will they leave it. I will write on them the name of my God and the name of the city of my God, the new Jerusalem, which is coming down out of heaven from my God; and I will also write on them my new name. ¹³ Whoever has ears, let them hear what the Spirit says to the churches.

The average size of a church in the USA is about 65–70 people, and about 70% of American churches have fewer than 100 people attending. Most of these churches spend disproportionate dollars on their buildings, and thus have bi-vocational or even volunteer pastors. Yet, small church America means a higher level of commitment. Just like Philadelphia, a modern city just off the highway on the road southeast from Sardis to Laodicea. Like so many small churches in the USA, Philadelphia's believers are faithful and resilient witnesses about Jesus. Philadelphia means "city of sibling love," but as Jeff Weima observes, the Christians were not experiencing their city as one of loving them (Weima, *Sermons*, 221–222).

Colossus Christ and His Commendation

The first words the Philadelphian believers hear from the Colossus Christ present to them a powerful image for a small church: Jesus is the "Devout One, the True One" (McKnight, *Second Testament*), the One who "holds the key of David," which means that "what he opens no one can shut" and "what he shuts no one can open" (3:7). These honorifics echo Isaiah so much one wonders if John had the prophet memorized (Isaiah 1:4; 22:22; 45:1; 60:14). And this Colossus Christ, who resounds always with the vision of Jesus in 1:9–20, knows their works (1:8a). Add to these descriptions the complaints of Jesus against the Jewish synagogue in Philadelphia in 3:9. When added, we recognize the descriptors of Jesus counter the claims of the Jewish leaders—namely, that they are devout and true and have the key. That Jesus uses "synagogue of Satan" indicates they have sided with

Babylon and the dragon and the wild things against those who witness to Jesus.

The Philadelphians get all commendation and no criticism. Unlike the other messages or letters, this commendation uses "I" seven times in the NIV to indicate that Jesus is watching them, knows them intimately, and is at work among them. The Colossus Christ (1) knows their works, and (2) provides for them an "open door," and (3) knows their powerlessness, and (4–5) will make those of the synagogue surrender to them, and (6) Jesus "loved" them, and (7) Jesus will preserve them "from the hour of trial" (3:8–10). Their works would have involved acts of compassion, love, and justice, as well as witnessing about and worshiping Jesus as Lord of lords. The "open door" could mean evangelistic opportunities (1 Corinthians 16:9) but more likely points to New Jerusalem's gates— they are wide open for these faithful Christians in this small church (cf. 3:12; 4:1; 21:25).

At #3 above I used "powerlessness" because Jesus literally says, "you have a little power," or "you have little power." Either they have a smidgeon of influence in Philadelphia, or this is a deliberate understatement, and they have none. Their lack of power glues itself to "yet you have kept my word and have not denied my name" (3:8). Small they may be, but, when the pressure came from the authorities in Philadelphia, they remained dissidents faithful to the Colossus Christ, the one who loved them, in their witness and worship. This same sense of resilience comes to the surface again in 3:10. Many Christians of the first century, and ever since, have been hauled before the authorities (cf. Matthew 10:18–20) who interrogate them about their behaviors and beliefs. In those moments the Spirit will not only guide their words but will also empower them to remain faithful. Their witnessing (*martureō*) before Babylon may lead to their witness as a martyrdom (*martus*). To these witnesses in Philadelphia, Jesus promises that they will be preserved from "the hour of trial," a trial that is global (3:10). That is, Jesus will guard them, protect them, and ultimately vindicate them. There is no promise here to escape either the trials of life or the final assault of the dragon against the people of God, namely, the children of the woman (12:17).

BABYLON CREEP AND CORRECTION

Philadelphia, like Smyrna, shows no signs of Babylon creeping in. So, the Colossus Christ, instead of piercing into their sinfulness, urges them to continue doing what they have been doing: "Hold on to what you have, so that no one will take your crown" (3:11). That is, "Grip what you have" and hold on tight because some hard times are coming (McKnight, *Second Testament*). What they have can be found in a re-reading of 3:8, 10.

CONSEQUENCES

Jesus uses a few images for their future in New Jerusalem. They will have a "crown" (3:11), they will become a "pillar in the temple of my God" (3:12) and they will never leave the temple of God (3:12). In addition, Jesus (notice again the "I") will "write on them the name of my God" as well as the "name of the city . . . New Jerusalem"—they will be its citizens—and Jesus will also "write on them my new name" (3:12; see 19:12). These graffiti-like inscriptions on their pillar in the temple, if you will, eternally counter what is written on the inhabitants of Babylon, what is often called the mark of the beast.

Unlike the lineups in so many of our church conferences where only the biggest churches are represented, only the best of worship bands play, and only the blueblood preachers speak, Jesus does not praise the biggest cities. Instead, his unequivocal affirmation goes to the church "with little power" and little numbers and little meetings. The measures we use—butts in seats, bills in the plate, baptisms in the water, and buildings on the campus—are not the measures of Jesus. He measures good works of compassion and justice, love for one another, faithfulness, and resilient witness in the face of the dragon.

QUESTIONS FOR REFLECTION AND APPLICATION

1. In what ways is the message to Philadelphia different from the other messages?

2. How does the powerlessness of the church in Philadelphia intersect with Jesus' protection?

3. What future awaits the small church of Philadelphia?

4. How big is your church? How do you feel about its size? How do you feel about its faithfulness?

5. How might Jesus measure the faithfulness of your church?

THE COMPROMISED CHURCH

Revelation 3:14–22

[14] "To the angel of the church in Laodicea write:

These are the words of the Amen, the faithful and true witness, the ruler of God's creation. [15] I know your deeds, that you are neither cold nor hot. I wish you were either one or the other! [16] So, because you are lukewarm—neither hot nor cold—I am about to spit you out of my mouth. [17] You say, 'I am rich; I have acquired wealth and do not need a thing.' But you do not realize that you are wretched, pitiful, poor, blind and naked. [18] I counsel you to buy from me gold refined in the fire, so you can become rich; and white clothes to wear, so you can cover your shameful nakedness; and salve to put on your eyes, so you can see.

[19] Those whom I love I rebuke and discipline. So be earnest and repent. [20] Here I am! I stand at the door and knock. If anyone hears my voice and opens the door, I will come in and eat with that person, and they with me.

[21] To the one who is victorious, I will give the right to sit with me on my throne, just as I was victorious and sat down with my

Father on his throne. ²² Whoever has ears, let them hear what the Spirit says to the churches."

Some people, sadly, are immunocompromised. The Penn Medicine website defines this condition this way:

> Think of your immune system as a strong army. Its mission? To protect you from enemies both foreign (viruses and bacteria) and domestic (diseases like cancer). But when you're immunocompromised, your immune system's defenses are low, affecting its ability to fight off infections and diseases.

The church of Laodicea, to invent an ugly word, was disciple-compromised. Jesus had nothing good to say about them because their allegiance to him had been so compromised by their allegiance to Babylon; they were in effect no longer following him. In the US, Christian nationalism hops the rails from Christians who are citizens to become a viewpoint that no longer distinguishes following Jesus from being an American patriot. That's not New Jerusalem; that's Babylon. Some progressive Christians are so committed to social justice through the federal government and activism that evangelism, Bible reading, foreign missions, and church participation no longer matter. That's not New Jerusalem; that's Babylon. Some businesspeople, some professional athletes, and some leadership gurus seem committed to the Christian faith only so it can increase their capital, their success on the court, or the size of their platform. That's not New Jerusalem; that's Babylon. These three illustrations of disciple-compromise correspond to what the Colossus Christ sees when he looks at Laodicea.

COLOSSUS CHRIST AND
HIS COMMENDATION

Jesus for the church in Laodicea is the "Amen" and "the faithful and true witness" and the "ruler of God's creation" (3:14). This is the only time in the book of Revelation Jesus is called the "Amen," but it echoes Isaiah 65's labeling of God as the Amen (65:16–17). The word "amen," used by us to close a prayer or to shout an agreement with someone, means "that's true" or "I agree." In Revelation 3:14, since it means "the One who is True," it connects tightly to "the faithful and true witness." Jesus saw, said, and suffered for what he saw and spoke. But he is also the "ruler of God's creation" because he is the King of kings and Lord of lords (1:5; 15:3; 17:14; 19:16) who stands over the "kings of the earth" who have surrendered their allegiance to Babylon (17:2, 9, 12, 18; 18:3, 9).

Pick up a pen and circle each instance of "I" when the "I" is the Colossus Christ in our passage. I count twelve instances in the NIV. Your translation may have more or fewer. Regardless of the number, Jesus is the one who sees and says in this passage. What he sees is not good, so what he says about the church of Laodicea is not good. Jesus does not commend Laodicea, which is even more noticeable because in the last passage about Philadelphia, Jesus had nothing bad to say.

Babylon Today: Opulence

In my book *Pastor Paul*, I wrote about the challenge of the church to form into a culture of generosity.

In doing that, I wrote about America's opulence in these words:

> About 75% of American garages have no cars in them because the car won't fit, while 90% of American garages are crammed with between 300 and 650 boxes of stuff. American homes are saturated with possessions, and this has all been revealingly detailed in statistics, stories, and high-quality images in *Life at Home in the Twenty-First Century* (Arnold, 23–51). Whenever I've talked about the subject of Christians and generosity, I hear a common pastoral observation: "I agree that Paul and the Bible teach economic justice, but what I find as a pastor is the need for so many in my church to learn how to manage their own money. So many are maxed out on their credit cards and loans, and many have no margin or are below water. What we need most is what Paul says about managing the money we've got with wisdom." Americans, in general, are gluttons for things. (McKnight, *Pastor Paul*, 89)

BABYLON CREEP AND CORRECTION

Once again, he begins with "I know your works [NIV has "deeds"]." The word "works" (*ergon*) also appears twelve times in the messages to the seven churches. Works express one's faith. Good works indicate—most of the time—sound faith; bad works indicate—most of the time—bad faith. Jesus sees and knows the make-up of the Christians and turns them inside out to say their works are vomitable. Jesus is not saying their works are lukewarm in that they are partly good and partly bad. No, he says their works are utterly useless.

The list of words describing why their works are vomitable is not short: their watery substance is "lukewarm," which mixes the refreshing cold waters from the Lycus River with the hot mineral waters coming from Hierapolis. Cold water is good; hot water is good; lukewarm water is useless. This good-for-neither becomes useless, spitworthy water. In some circles, the notion of lukewarm is exploited to get teens to go all-in for God. Jon Ward, in his recent book *Testimony*, speaks of such an experience and points out that some leaders used the threat and fear of lukewarmness to "promote absolutism" (Ward, *Testimony*, 53). Ward is right. I heard the message as a teen dozens of times. I advise caution in the use of the idea of lukewarmness. We should always connect it not so much to commitment as to the quality and usefulness of our works.

The Laodiceans presume on being like so much of Laodicea, "rich" (17:3–4) and, like Babylon, that they "do not need a thing" (18:7). Instead of good works, instead of genuine riches, the Colossus Christ reveals that they are "wretched, pitiful, poor, blind and naked" (3:17). The five words combine to contrast their presumptuous Babylon arrogance and vanity with the reality of their spiritual condition. The reputation for Laodicea was its wealth. So wealthy were they that, in 60 AD, when an earthquake hit, the city refused the financial assistance of Rome's vast resources. The believers had been sucked into Laodicean Babylon-like vanity.

Jesus sticks with his network of metaphors. To repent

he tells them "to buy from me gold refined in the fire, so you can become rich; and white clothes to wear, so you can cover your shameful nakedness; and salve to put on your eyes, so you can see" (3:18). Laodicea was famous for its banking institutions, its medical facilities, and for its eye salve, so Jesus plays on their local context. But the expressions remain metaphorical and they, once interpreted, mean, *Turn to me. Repent. Do the works of a gospel-shaped life. Be witnesses and worship the Lamb.*

Jesus reminds them, in a theme found in all the prophets, that "I convince and discipline as many as I love" (3:19; McKnight, *Second Testament*). Jesus does not toss Laodicea under the bus. He loves that church but knows its only way forward out of its vanity and arrogance is the discipline of a radical repentance, revival, and reformation.

CONSEQUENCES

Jesus overpowers his criticisms of Laodicea with his love and offer of grace. Not only is discipline an act of love, but he offers to come dine with them and now stands at their door awaiting their reception (3:20). While this famous verse has been used over and over in evangelism, where it has proven more than helpful, its original context was for believers hopping back into the lane of faithful discipleship. The disciple-compromised condition can be healed simply by sitting at the table with Jesus. Not only does he promise meals with him, Jesus promises they will—a la Matthew 19:28—get to "sit with me on my throne" (Revelation 3:21). As Jesus was a faithful witness to the bitter end and was raised to sit with the Father, so the Laodiceans get the invitation to walk with Jesus out of their Babylon lifestyle into the way of the Lamb that leads to the New Jerusalem.

QUESTIONS FOR REFLECTION
AND APPLICATION

1. What does it mean when a church is "disciple-compromised"?

2. When Jesus is called the "Amen," what does that entail?

3. What is the relationship between works and faith?

4. How have you heard "lukewarmness" taught in the past? How does this corrective perspective about usefulness impact you?

5. In what ways might your allegiance to Jesus be compromised by your allegiance to a political power?

FOR FURTHER READING

Jeanne E. Arnold, et al., *Life at Home in the Twenty-First Century: Thirty-Two Families Open Their Doors* (Los Angeles: The Cotsen Institute of Archaeology Press, 2017), 23–51.

Penn Medicine site: https://www.pennmedicine.org/updates/blogs/health-and-wellness/2020/may/what-it-means-to-be-immunocompromised.

Jon Ward, *Testimony* (Grand Rapids: Brazos Press, 2023).

Scot McKnight, *Pastor Paul: Nurturing a Culture of Christoformity in the Church* (Grand Rapids: Brazos Press, 2019), quoting p. 89.

The Playbill of Revelation: Who Does What in This Drama?

Team Dragon in Babylon

BABYLON Mission is to embody the way of the dragon. Rides on the wild thing. Characterized by royalty, idolatry, opulence, murder, status, arrogance, power, military might, murder, and economic exploitation. Kills those in the way of the Lamb. Gathers under her power the kings of the earth, merchants of the world, and sea captains. Serves as a timeless metaphor for empire and injustices and idolatries. In John's day, Babylon is Rome. Babylon falls. Also known as the great prostitute.

THE DRAGON Has a mission of accusation, deceit, death. Chases the woman but loses her. Wages war with the woman's children. Battles Michael the angel and loses. Has control of the wild things, significant control with the political powers embodied in Babylon. Defeated by the Lamb and by the allegiant witnesses. Bound for one thousand years, released, and then destroyed in the lake of fire. Also known as Satan, the devil.

WILD THING #1 (FROM SEA) Mission is to embody the will of the dragon. Represents chaos, power, deception, and opposition to the Lamb. Ruler of evil empires. One of the dead-heads of the wild thing is raised from the dead. Worshiped by humans. Its rule is temporary. Makes up one third of the unholy trinity: dragon, wild thing #1 and #2. Aka the beast from the sea.

WILD THING #2 (FROM EARTH) Mission is to embody the will of wild thing #1 and dragon. The sycophant in chief, the propagandist. Looks like the Lamb, acts like the dragon. Forces worship of wild thing #1, does fraudulent miracles, deceives the world. Forces humans to accept the "mark of the wild thing." Its name is its number, 666. Aka the beast from the earth.

666 Represents Roman Emperor Nero and many others.

OTHERS Jezebel and the Nicolaitans/Nicolaus and Balaam. These are representative names, serving as stereotypes for idolatries and sexual immoralities and false teachings.

Team Lamb in New Jerusalem

GOD ON THE THRONE The God of Israel, the Father, the sovereign God over all, who orchestrates the events of history toward the New Jerusalem. God's might is matched by God's gracious love. This God will defeat the dragon, banish death, and establish life in New Jerusalem. To God belongs all worship and praise and honor and glory because this God brings salvation through the Lamb. Trinity: Father, Son (Lamb), and Spirit.

THE SEVEN SPIRITS Though some question this, the Seven Spirits are John's language for the Holy Spirit. The number represents perfection or completeness, and it corresponds to the missions of the Spirit.

THE LAMB In the center of the throne room and the center of the action in Revelation. The Lamb is the Lord Jesus Christ, who has many names and attributes, including: Jesus, Messiah, faithful witness, first born from among the dead, ruler of the kings of the earth, loves us, liberates us, Alpha and Omega, who is, who was, who is to come, like a son of man, first and last, living one, holds keys of death and Hades. Lion, Lamb, Logos, Light: all of these represent the Lord over all lords and King over all kings. He is the Savior/Redeemer by his blood.

THE ALLEGIANT WITNESSES These are the believers and followers of Jesus in the way of the Lamb. The seven churches are faithful (allegiant) witnesses in life and word to the way of the Lamb and the rule of King Jesus. They suffer for their witness. They are known for their works of goodness and love and kindness.

THE WOMAN She appears to morph in Revelation 12 from Eve to Israel to Mary, mother of Jesus, and finally to the church. She is opposed by the dragon, who tries to kill her and the baby boy born to her (Jesus). She escapes under protection from God. Her offspring is opposed by the dragon.

ENVOYS/ANGELS Abundant in Revelation, they perform missions for God in this world for the redemption of humans.

TWENTY-FOUR ELDERS They surround the throne, wearing white clothing with gold crowns. The number twenty-four suggests two times twelve, representing Israel and the apostles. Altogether they represent the redeemed people of God in worship of God.

FOUR LIVING THINGS They surround the throne, cover their eyes, have six wings, and praise God endlessly. They intercede, and at times guide John through the three times seven judgments/disciplines. They echo the living creatures of Isaiah 6 and Ezekiel 1's four living things and represent all creation worshiping God.

MYRIADS Those who worship God are innumerable.

NEW JERUSALEM This future, ideal city is the world as God designed it to be. It is inhabited by those who want to dwell in God's presence and with whom God dwells. It is better than the visions of the Greco-Roman visions of society (Plato, Aristotle, Cicero), it fulfills the expectations of Israel's prophets and more, and it takes the old Jerusalem and becomes the heaven-with-us kingdom of God. (McKnight-Matchett, *RRU*, 38–39)

THE EMPIRE'S TRUE GOD

Revelation 4:1–11

¹ After this I looked, and there before me was a door standing open in heaven. And the voice I had first heard speaking to me like a trumpet said, "Come up here, and I will show you what must take place after this." ² At once I was in the Spirit, and there before me was a throne in heaven with someone sitting on it. ³ And the one who sat there had the appearance of jasper and ruby. A rainbow that shone like an emerald encircled the throne. ⁴ Surrounding the throne were twenty-four other thrones, and seated on them were twenty-four elders. They were dressed in white and had crowns of gold on their heads. ⁵ From the throne came flashes of lightning, rumblings and peals of thunder. In front of the throne, seven lamps were blazing. These are the seven spirits of God. ⁶ Also in front of the throne there was what looked like a sea of glass, clear as crystal.

In the center, around the throne, were four living creatures, and they were covered with eyes, in front and in back. ⁷ The first living creature was like a lion, the second was like an ox, the third had a face like a man, the fourth was like a flying eagle. ⁸ Each of the four living creatures had six wings and was covered with eyes all around, even under its wings. Day and night they never stop saying:

> " 'Holy, holy, holy
>   is the Lord God Almighty,'
> who was, and is, and is to come."

⁹ *Whenever the living creatures give glory, honor and thanks to him who sits on the throne and who lives for ever and ever,* ¹⁰ *the twenty-four elders fall down before him who sits on the throne and worship him who lives for ever and ever. They lay their crowns before the throne and say:*

> ¹¹ *"You are worthy, our Lord and God,
>   to receive glory and honor and power,
> for you created all things,
>   and by your will they were created
> and have their being."*

The book of Revelation has to be read in chunks. Read Revelation 1 and reflect. Then read all of Revelation 2–3 and reflect. Then Revelation 4–5, the first chapter concentrating our attention on the glory of the "Lord God Almighty," and the second chapter on the worthiness of the Lamb to open the scroll so he can break the seals of judgments against injustice (more on this later). What the believers in the seven churches perceive as they listen to chapter four being read is that, though Domitian is on the throne in Rome, though his local agents curry his favor and do what they want to John, the author of this Apocalypse, and though they experience routine harassment and even persecution, *they can know that their God is on the Throne.*

The Christians of western Asia Minor don't have to wait for chapter seventeen to hear about Babylon. They know her face in the day-to-day. When they hear this chapter read and catch the beat of the two snatches of songs (4:8, 11) their hearts swell with confidence that someday justice will be established.

Ian Paul asks the questions that today's passage must have evoked for the believers in western Asia Minor: "Why worry about temporary opposition, whether from Jews or pagans, if God is truly enthroned and all powerful? Why compromise with surrounding culture when the patterns of authority there are just a shadow of the reality of God's authority? And why falter and stumble if this vision represents your inheritance and your destiny?" (Paul, *Revelation*, 120).

INSIDE INFORMATION

In chapter one John gets a revelation from God when he hears and then sees (1:10, 12, 17, 19). In chapter four John opens with the visionary "I saw" but he grabs his listeners' attention with a sudden "Look!" (untranslated in the NIV). What he saw and wanted his listeners to imagine was "a door standing open in heaven" (4:1). But he gets more than a vision of a door. The trumpet-voice, the very voice of Jesus himself that he heard and saw in chapter one, orders John to "Come up here!" where he will receive inside information, which is what apocalypses are all about: "what must take place after this."

The experience of hearing inside information corresponds quite well with what John experiences. In fact, the rest of the book of Revelation records John's inside information. John not only was given information that passed over the desk of God and on to Jesus and then on to an angel and then finally to him, but John rode the Spirit elevator to the very throne room of God to see and hear things himself. Apocalypse is about unveiling what had been veiled, and what was unveiled is inside information.

How one gets from Patmos to the threshold of heaven requires an explanation, and John does not disappoint: "At once I was in the Spirit" (4:2). Like the experience of staring at an autostereogram,* where flat dots and images morph into 3D, John in the Spirit peers through the veil of earthly life into the throne room of heaven. What John saw was what his listeners wanted to know: *What did you see, John?* He now answers that question.

Babylon Today: Church decline

Bob Smietana, among America's finest writers about religion, observes:

> A recent survey from Pew Religion, released in late 2021, found that three out of every ten Americans (29%) is a so-called None, someone who claims no identity—up from only 16% in 2007. The percentage of Christians had also dropped, from 78 percent to 63 percent over the same time frame. Earlier in the year, Gallup announced that for the first time since the 1940s, less than half of

---

* https://en.wikipedia.org/wiki/Autostereogram.

Americans claimed to be a member of a house of worship.

American religion is in a time of unprecedented transformation.

For most of its history, America has been a mostly white, mostly Christian nation, run mostly by men and where conservative Christian ideas about sex and marriage and money and morals ruled the day. Organized religion was a powerful and well-respected force, and other social institutions often deferred to religious leaders and gave Christians a place of honor and respect.

All that has changed. The country is rapidly becoming a multi-ethnic, pluralistic, egalitarian nation, where women and men are increasingly seen as equal, where traditional ideas about the nuclear family have been replaced by a more inclusive, LGBT-affirming view of sex and marriage, and where the fastest growing religious group in the country are the so-called Nones—those who claim no religious affiliation. (Smietana, *Reorganized Religion*, xv, 9)

THE THRONE AND ITS GOD

John, as you are now accustomed to reading, is filled with images and metaphors and abstractions. In Revelation 4 John sees the throne room and describes it in terms that evoke as much as, if not more than, he describes.

First, John sees a throne and, second, he sees "someone [God] sitting on it" (4:2). Emperors and kings sit on thrones.

Babylon has an emperor, Domitian. But heaven has another emperor, the world's true king, God. Precious stones, like the jasper and ruby and emerald of 4:3, sparkle and flash frequently in the Apocalypse. The New Jerusalem's wall was made of jasper, the fourth foundation of emerald, and the sixth foundation was of ruby (21:18–20). In chapter four, however, John perceives God on the throne as one having the "appearance" of jasper (reddish-brown) and ruby (or carnelian), while the rainbow encompassing the throne was like emerald. The One sitting on the throne is none other than "the Lord God Almighty" or "our Lord and God" (4:8, 11).

Believers in any of these seven churches would have been daily familiar with shrines and temples dedicated to prayers for and worship of the emperor. Revelation 4 counters those temples and worship, revealing the ultimate inside information that the only true God on the throne is God, Father of the Lord Jesus Christ.

The Nine Songs of Revelation

Revelation 4:8–11;* 5:8–14;* 7:9–12;* 11:15–18;* 12:10–12; 15:2–4; 16:5–7;* 19:1–4;* 19:5–8

Those marked with an asterisk are antiphonal, that is, with one group singing and another responding back with their own lines. These songs have shaped the hymns of the church, but they also resemble in very important ways the Negro Spirituals tradition. To sing these songs as an act

of resistance, even if at times it takes eyes to see
and ears to hear the notes of dissidence in them.
In which case, the songs can be understood as Call
and Response.

Brian Blount comments:

> The hymns of Revelation, then, are a celebration
> of confrontational resistance. John's hearers and
> readers live in an oppressive climate where they
> will be punished for standing up and standing
> out against the lordship of Rome. These hymns
> incite them to respond to the eschatological
> worship call of angels, cherubim, elders, and a
> heavenly multitude of souls with their own politi-
> cally charged worship and witness to history's sole
> sovereign—to the almighty God and to the Lamb.
> (Blound, *Revelation*, 95–98)

AROUND THE THRONE

John's eyes must have been dancing and shifting the
way one's eyes move in REM sleep. Notice these terms:
"Surrounding the throne" and "from the throne" and "In
front of the throne" and "around the throne" (4:4–6). John
gets lost in the wonder of the adoring praise of God by the
inhabitants of the throne room. John sees:

1. twenty-four elders sitting on twenty-four thrones
   that encircle the throne, and they are suited in the
   whites of purity and wore crowns of gold (4:4);
2. flashes of both lightning and thunder (4:5), as in
   Exodus 19:18–21;

3. seven flaming lamps (on lampstands?) before the throne, which John interprets as the seven Spirits of God (4:5);

4. a crystal-clear sea of glass in front of the throne (4:6);

5. and in the middle encircling the throne were "four living creatures" covered with all-direction-seeing eyes—like a lion, ox, face of a human, a flying eagle—and each also had six wings which were also covered with all-direction-seeing eyes (4:6b-9). These sound like Ezekiel 1:5–25 or Isaiah 6:1–4, or both!

It does not help to turn these into literal beings. What John describes mixes the common with the grotesque, and his language takes us where we need to go. Why are there twenty-four? An old answer remains the most likely: they are the sum of twelve tribes of Israel and twelve apostles. John chose, however, not to identify who they are, and it remains even better to stick with his choice.

The throne room of God, in a way vastly superior to the throne rooms of emperors of Rome or kings of nations, is surrounded not by sycophants but by the praise of all creation. Pondering such a scene, we join St. Francis of Assisi's wonderful hymn, "All Creatures of our God and King," and join the inhabitants of heaven's throne room in praise to our great God.**

All (four living) creatures sing their lines, perhaps in four-part harmony, and then the twenty-four elders sing their lines antiphonally. We might not be overdoing it if we wonder if this isn't a back-and-forth of ceaseless praise

---

** https://hymnary.org/hymn/HHOF1980/12.

throughout all eternity. John tells us, at least, the four living creatures are doing this "day and night they never stop" (4:8), and that a summary of their song is "glory, honor and thanks" (4:9). The four living creatures attribute a thrice-holy to the "Lord God Almighty," and then describe God as the One who "was, and is, and is to come" (cf. 1:4).

When the four living creature's words are completed, the twenty-four elders "fall down" before the One on the throne and they "lay their crowns before the throne" to praise the One who alone is "worthy . . . to receive glory and honor and power," words that echo in antiphony the words of the four living creatures. The basis of the praise of the twenty-four elders is that God both creates all creatures and sustains all creation (4:11).

To sing out antiphonally that "You are worthy" is an act of dissidence against the one thought worthy in the Roman empire, namely, the emperor. Worship in the book of Revelation is an act of subversion and resistance. Those praising God as the true Lord of lords could not then give glory and honor to the emperor or even to local magistrates. As Ian Paul asked at the top of today's reflection, "Why worry? Why compromise? Why falter and stumble?"

QUESTIONS FOR REFLECTION AND APPLICATION

1. What is the heart of the inside information John sees in his apocalypse and communicates to the churches?

2. For the Christians of Asia Minor, how might their context of being surrounded with glittering altars and temples have impacted their understanding of John's apocalypse?

3. How might the scenes of worshiping the Lamb on the throne have differed from the scenes of idol worship and emperor worship John's recipients would have been familiar with?

4. What do you think of the idea of worship as subversion and resistance?

5. What worship song or hymn lyrics can you think of that might be subversive to your surrounding culture?

FOR FURTHER READING

Bob Smietana, *Reorganized Religion: The Reshaping of the American Church and Why It Matters* (New York: Worthy, 2022), quoting pp. xv, 9.

THE LAMB WHO
IS A LION

Revelation 5:1–14

¹ Then I saw in the right hand of him who sat on the throne a scroll with writing on both sides and sealed with seven seals. ² And I saw a mighty angel proclaiming in a loud voice, "Who is worthy to break the seals and open the scroll?" ³ But no one in heaven or on earth or under the earth could open the scroll or even look inside it. ⁴ I wept and wept because no one was found who was worthy to open the scroll or look inside. ⁵ Then one of the elders said to me, "Do not weep! See, the Lion of the tribe of Judah, the Root of David, has triumphed. He is able to open the scroll and its seven seals."

⁶ Then I saw a Lamb, looking as if it had been slain, standing at the center of the throne, encircled by the four living creatures and the elders. The Lamb had seven horns and seven eyes, which are the seven spirits of God sent out into all the earth. ⁷ He went and took the scroll from the right hand of him who sat on the throne. ⁸ And when he had taken it, the four living creatures and the twenty-four elders fell down before the Lamb. Each one had a harp and they were holding golden bowls full of incense, which are the prayers of God's people. ⁹ And they sang a new song, saying:

"You are worthy to take the scroll
and to open its seals,
because you were slain,
and with your blood you purchased for God
persons from every tribe and language and people
and nation.
10 You have made them to be a kingdom and priests to
serve our God,
and they will reign on the earth."
11 Then I looked and heard the voice of many angels,
numbering thousands upon thousands, and ten
thousand times ten thousand. They encircled the
throne and the living creatures and the elders. 12
In a loud voice they were saying:
"Worthy is the Lamb, who was slain,
to receive power and wealth and wisdom and
strength
and honor and glory and praise!"
13 Then I heard every creature in heaven and on earth
and under the earth and on the sea, and all that
is in them, saying:
"To him who sits on the throne and to the Lamb
be praise and honor and glory and power,
for ever and ever!"
14 The four living creatures said, "Amen," and the
elders fell down and worshiped.

God on heaven's throne surrounded by ceaseless worship electrifies the seven churches. Until they leave the assembly and walk home through the streets that remind them daily that Domitian is on the throne. What they need is more than a bald claim that God is on the throne. What they need is for justice to rain down on western Asia Minor. What they need is a new emperor, a King over all kings, and a Lord over all the lordless lords of this world. Revelation 5 will open the door, or rather, open the scroll to that possibility for the believers. I join Gordon Fee who opens his comments on today's passage with words that tell my own experience: "With these words John sets the scene for one of the great moments in all known literature. Indeed, so remarkable is the vision that an interpreter is made to pause and wonder whether his or her own words, in trying to comment on it all, might not get in the way of its splendor" (Fee, *Revelation*, 75).

The oddity of Revelation 5 is that we Bible readers know too much. So, we need to read slowly to notice that what happens in this chapter are these items: the One on the throne has a scroll and needs someone to break its seven seals to discover what's in it. Which leads to "What's in it?" Chapter five does not tell us. What it does tell us is that Jesus, the Lion who is the Lamb, or the Lamb who is the Lion, is worthy to open the scroll. Before he opens the scroll, however, the choirs of heaven erupt in four antiphonal songs to praise the Lamb who is the Lion. What they sing about is the Lamb's redemption of a new community, the Lamb's glory, and the Lamb's occupation of the throne next to the One on the throne.

Leaving us to ask again, What's in the scroll? (We have to wait until chapter six.)

QUEST

Both Revelation four and five fit the bill for an apocalypse. They both reveal to us inside information. Chapter four was about God on the throne, and chapter five's inside information is about an unopened scroll, teasing us all into wondering what's written inside. Some "mighty angel" announces in its preacher voice a question for all those in heaven: "Who is worthy to break the seals and open the scroll?" Not a soul in heaven has a clue who could be worthy, which implies none of the groups we've met so far—angels, twenty-four elders, and four living creatures—are worthy. But the voice of the angel extends out of heaven to earth and even "under" the earth. Still, no one worthy. John's response: "I was wailing much because no one was found deserving either to open the book or to see it" (5:4; McKnight, *Second Testament*).

An unstated set of assumptions drive the scene, including the assumption that God's holding a scroll with seven seals that needs to be opened; the assumption that what is written in that scroll matters for John, for the seven churches, and for justice. Those assumptions, and more besides, emerge so deep from John's heart that the absence of someone worthy makes him wail like a prophet.

DISCOVERY

But one of the elders urges John to stop wailing because he has discovered someone who can open the scroll. The elder says, "Look! The Lion" from the tribe of Judah, which is the tribal "Root of David," has triumphed. He has conquered and can "open the scroll and its seven seals" (5:5). The quest of the angel and John is over: they have discovered one who is worthy. The images at work in "Lion" and "Judah" and "David" point us to a powerful figure, perhaps a Rome-like military commander who can win on the battlefield and return to Rome with a triumphant parade all the way to the Forum.

It's good that our Bibles have at least a paragraph break because what comes next is a stunner.

Morphing

The Lion disappears and John reveals to us that he "saw a Lamb," not a Lion, not a David-like figure. And the Lamb he saw appeared to have "been slain." Yet, the slain Lamb has "seven horns and seven eyes, which are the seven spirits of God sent out into all the earth" (5:6). A lot happens here. The Lion sets up an image of immense, irresistible, terrifying power. The Lion morphs in John's narrative into a slain Lamb. We all know this means Jesus who was crucified and raised. The One worthy to open the scrolls and unleash divine judgment against evil and establish justice is the Crucified One. Not an emperor with a sword in his fist but a blood-stained Lamb. The One who will conquer evil will not do so by violence but by a Word-based sword that will slay with the goodness of the gospel. A mixed metaphor, to be sure. The Lamb's seven horns will best the Wild Thing's ten horns (13:1). But, not with a sword in his fist as in Christian nationalism but with a Sword-Mouth that slays evil with the Word of God.

Babylon Today: Christian Nationalism

Andrew Whitehead and Samuel Perry define Christian nationalism as:

> A cultural framework—a collection of myths, traditions, symbols, narratives, and value systems—that idealizes and advocates a fusion of Christianity with American civic life . . . the "Christianity" of

Christian nationalism represents something more than religion. As we will show, it includes assumptions of nativism, white supremacy, patriarchy, and heteronormativity, along with divine sanction for authoritarian control and militarism. It is as ethnic and political as it is religious. (Whitehead, Perry, *Taking America Back*, 10)

A more recent study by Samuel Perry, with Philip Gorski, examines not only Christian nationalism's gluing of church/religion and state, but recognizes America's gluing of white supremacy and racism to Christian nationalism. They offer this American narrative of white Christian nationalism, and they know this ideology has a secularism version that is as important at times as the so-called "Christian" version:

America was founded as a Christian nation by white men who were traditional Christians who based the nation's founding documents on Christian principles. The United States is blessed by God, which is why it has been so successful; And the nation has a special role to play in God's plan for humanity. But these blessings are threatened by cultural degradation from unamerican influences both inside and outside our borders. (Gorski, *The Flag*, 4, 6)

This is a culture clutch of Americans, and their voting reveals the clutch: "contemporary proponents of white Christian nationalism also hold strong views on many other issues, including racial discrimination, religious freedom, government regulation, socialism, the welfare state, COVID lockdowns, voting, and the capitol insurrection."

Their sketch of Christian nationalism reveals it is not the same as patriotism, white evangelicalism, and it is not (ironically) just something found among white evangelical *Christians*. Secularists have joined the culture clutch.

Somehow the Lamb, which we all know doesn't even have hands, "took the scroll from the right hand of"—notice how impossible it is for John to describe God Almighty— "him who sat on the throne" (5:7). We still don't know what's in that scroll. John would rather describe the praises of heaven before he reveals the breaking of those seals.

THE ANTIPHONIES

We now encounter four antiphonal responses to the discovery of the Lamb who is worthy. But, as Fee says it so well, "what follows is intended to be something of a diorama to be visualized rather than a text simply to be read, even though it comes to his readers in words" (Fee, *Revelation*, 78). Use your imagination; go where these songs take you. Look. Listen. Feel. Taste. Touch. And above all, don't rush through the reading of the text. In reading, find a quiet place where you can chant or sing aloud these words. They work best when we use our voices and raise our arms in praise. Imagine, too, believers in the seven churches gathering with the musicians in a corner to figure out how best to raise these words a notch or two into music.

Remember the first words of this Book? "The Revelation [of] Jesus Christ," which we said could be translated "Jesus-Christ Revelation." The NIV has "from Jesus Christ" and it could be a revelation "about" Jesus Christ. Yes, both. Amen? In Revelation 5 we see why it can be translated a revelation *about* Jesus Christ. Jesus, the Lamb who is a Lion, is the center of attention from this point forward.

FOUR LIVING CREATURES AND THE TWENTY-FOUR ELDERS

In response to the Lamb's trotters somehow grasping the scroll, John watches the four living creatures and the twenty-four elders (=4+24) fall down in worship before the Lamb (5:8). Right there one encounters the reality of God's throne room: all creatures great and small are overwhelmed, in body and spirit, in the presence of the glory of God and the Lamb. Each of the 4+24 was in possession of two items to express their worship, both of which are physical expressions of worship: a kithara (NIV has "harp" but that's too large) and a golden bowl full of incense that represents the "prayers of God's people," who are praying for the kind of justice that is found in New Jerusalem (5:8).

The song of the 4+24 has four themes, but as you read these four themes notice the progression: first, that the Lamb alone in all of heaven is "worthy," or "deserving" to open the scroll and to break the seals so all will know what will happen to the dragon's social institution, Babylon. Second, the Lamb is worthy because, by the Lamb's death (= "blood") he "purchased" out of Babylon, in order to present to God, persons "from every tribe and language and people and nation." John likes the wideness of God's redemptive work (cf. 7:9; 10:11; 11:9; 13:7; 14:6; 17:15).

Ponder how the minuscule size of the churches were to the scope of this heavenly vision. Third, the Lamb's redemption transforms ordinary sinners into a "kingdom of priests to serve our God." The highest religious status one could achieve in the Roman empire as well as in the Jewish world was to be a priest. *All on Team Lamb* are priests. And, fourth, the Lamb's redeemed priests will also be kings because they "will reign on the earth" (5:9–10). The ordinary believers in the seven churches are revealed the inside information that they, yes, they, will replace the Roman emperor as an entire people who will be the rulers under the rule of the Lord of lords and King of kings.

MYRIADS OF ANGELS

In response to the 4+24 John both sees and hears "the voice of many angels," and he realizes the word "many" will not do it. So he corrects himself by adding nuance about those he sees who "encircled the throne" and 4+24. His scanner finds "thousands upon thousands, and ten thousand times ten thousand" (5:11). This is first century for *infinity*. As Ellen Davis wrote about the angels' song in 5:11–12, "For sheer fanfare, there's nothing quite like it in the whole Bible" (Davis, *Preaching the Word*, 310).

Their antiphonal response to the 4+24 is captivated only with the first lines of the 4+24 song. They sing only about the worthiness of the Lamb, "who was slain," but instead of pressing into his worthiness to open the scroll, they find him worthy "to receive power and wealth and wisdom and strength and honor and glory and praise!" (5:12). These terms, or a combination of them, is seen elsewhere (e.g., 4:11; 7:12; 19:1). This is the standard language of early Christian praise choruses! Those who have read Revelation 17–19's description of Babylon will recognize that *all Babylon sought and desired* was glory and honor but those with inside information now know *it will all go to the Lamb.* The dragon's Babylon will someday lose its glory, and God will reroute the worship of the world toward the Lamb of God.

EVERY CREATURE IN ALL OF HEAVEN AND EARTH

I never read Revelation 5:13's "every creature in heaven and on earth and under the earth and on the sea" without thinking of the last chapter of C.S. Lewis's *The Last Battle* where all the inhabitants of Narnia gather at the door to be ushered into a kind of Narnia well beyond the ordinary Narnia. Where all adore Aslan. The "every creature" song in antiphony to the angels in antiphony to the 4+24 expresses simple, powerful doxology, which means "words of glory": "To him who sits on the throne and to the Lamb be praise and honor and glory and power, for ever and ever!" (5:13). Imagine the praise of the ruby-throated hummingbird, the wood duck, the muskrat, the squirrel, and the opossum. It's like Noah's ark suddenly erupting into a worship night.

THE FOUR LIVING CREATURES AND THE TWENTY-FOUR ELDERS

How to sing as an antiphony to the words of the angels and creatures? One word, uttered by the four living creatures, does it: "Amen!" The last antiphonal response, a wordless response, is "the elders fell down and worshiped" (5:14).

To see God and the Lamb enthroned in heaven elicits by everyone the feeling of being overwhelmed by goodness and glory and majesty and awe and adoration and most especially love. A love so enraptured with God's majestic grace that the body falls down in gratitude—just to be there singing along with all creation.

The book of Revelation, it has been said by many, is all about worship. The two major words for discipleship in Revelation are witness and worship. To worship the Lamb turns from the imperial cult of worshiping the emperor. To worship the Lamb resists Babylon and those who do this become dissidents of the dragon. Worshiping the Lamb, let this be said over and over, subverts all other gods.

QUESTIONS FOR REFLECTION AND APPLICATION

1. What emotions do you notice in this scene? What emotions does it stir in you?

2. What makes the Lion/Lamb worthy to open the scroll?

3. Why is it significant that all of the people on the Lamb's team are priests?

4. As you try to imagine this scene, what surprises or intrigues you?

5. What prayers or songs evoke in you the same sense of worship that this scene communicates?

FOR FURTHER READING

Philip S. Gorski, Samuel L. Perry, foreword by Jemar Tisby, *The Flag and the Cross: White Christian Nationalism and the Threat to American Democracy* (New York: Oxford University Press, 2022), quoting pp. 4, 6.

Andrew Whitehead, Samuel Perry, *Taking America Back for God: Christian Nationalism in the United States* (New York: Oxford University Press, 2020), quoting p. 10.

THE PLOT OF JUSTICE

Revelation 6:1–8:1

^{6:1} *I watched as the Lamb opened the first of the seven seals. Then I heard one of the four living creatures say in a voice like thunder, "Come!"* ² *I looked, and there before me was a white horse! Its rider held a bow, and he was given a crown, and he rode out as a conqueror bent on conquest.*

³ *When the Lamb opened the second seal, I heard the second living creature say, "Come!"* ⁴ *Then another horse came out, a fiery red one. Its rider was given power to take peace from the earth and to make people kill each other. To him was given a large sword.*

⁵ *When the Lamb opened the third seal, I heard the third living creature say, "Come!" I looked, and there before me was a black horse! Its rider was holding a pair of scales in his hand.* ⁶ *Then I heard what sounded like a voice among the four living creatures, saying, "Two pounds of wheat for a day's wages, and six pounds of barley for a day's wages, and do not damage the oil and the wine!"*

⁷ *When the Lamb opened the fourth seal, I heard the voice of the fourth living creature say, "Come!"* ⁸ *I looked, and there before me was a pale horse! Its rider was named Death, and*

Hades was following close behind him. They were given power over a fourth of the earth to kill by sword, famine and plague, and by the wild beasts of the earth.

⁹ **When he opened the fifth seal, I saw under the altar the souls of those who had been slain because of the word of God and the testimony they had maintained.** ¹⁰ **They called out in a loud voice, "How long, Sovereign Lord, holy and true, until you judge the inhabitants of the earth and avenge our blood?"** ¹¹ **Then each of them was given a white robe, and they were told to wait a little longer, until the full number of their fellow servants, their brothers and sisters, were killed just as they had been.**

¹² *I watched as he opened the sixth seal. There was a great earthquake. The sun turned black like sackcloth made of goat hair, the whole moon turned blood red,* ¹³ *and the stars in the sky fell to earth, as figs drop from a fig tree when shaken by a strong wind.* ¹⁴ *The heavens receded like a scroll being rolled up, and every mountain and island was removed from its place.*

¹⁵ *Then the kings of the earth, the princes, the generals, the rich, the mighty, and everyone else, both slave and free, hid in caves and among the rocks of the mountains.* ¹⁶ *They called to the mountains and the rocks, "Fall on us and hide us from the face of him who sits on the throne and from the wrath of the Lamb!* ¹⁷ *For the great day of their wrath has come, and who can withstand it?"*

⁷:¹ **After this I saw four angels standing at the four corners of the earth, holding back the four winds of the earth to prevent any wind from blowing on the land or on the sea or on any tree.** ² **Then I saw another angel coming up from the east, having the seal of the living God. He called out in a loud voice to the four angels who had been given power to harm the land and the sea:** ³ **"Do not harm the land or the sea or the trees until we put a seal on the foreheads**

of the servants of our God." ⁴ *Then I heard the number of those who were sealed: 144,000 from all the tribes of Israel.*

> ⁵ *From the tribe of Judah 12,000 were sealed,*
> *from the tribe of Reuben 12,000,*
> *from the tribe of Gad 12,000,*
> ⁶ *from the tribe of Asher 12,000,*
> *from the tribe of Naphtali 12,000,*
> *from the tribe of Manasseh 12,000,*
> ⁷ *from the tribe of Simeon 12,000,*
> *from the tribe of Levi 12,000,*
> *from the tribe of Issachar 12,000,*
> ⁸ *from the tribe of Zebulun 12,000,*
> *from the tribe of Joseph 12,000,*
> *from the tribe of Benjamin 12,000.*

⁹ *After this I looked, and there before me was a great multitude that no one could count, from every nation, tribe, people and language, standing before the throne and before the Lamb. They were wearing white robes and were holding palm branches in their hands.* ¹⁰ *And they cried out in a loud voice:*

> *"Salvation belongs to our God,*
> *who sits on the throne,*
> *and to the Lamb."*

¹¹ *All the angels were standing around the throne and around the elders and the four living creatures. They fell down on their faces before the throne and worshiped God,* ¹² *saying:*

> *"Amen!*
> *Praise and glory*

and wisdom and thanks and honor
and power and strength
be to our God for ever and ever.
Amen!"

[13] *Then one of the elders asked me, "These in white robes—who are they, and where did they come from?"*
[14] *I answered, "Sir, you know."*
And he said, "These are they who have come out of the great tribulation; they have washed their robes and made them white in the blood of the Lamb. [15] *Therefore,*

"they are before the throne of God
and serve him day and night in his temple;
and he who sits on the throne
will shelter them with his presence.
[16] *'Never again will they hunger;*
never again will they thirst.
The sun will not beat down on them,'
nor any scorching heat.
[17] *For the Lamb at the center of the throne*
will be their shepherd;
'he will lead them to springs of living water.'
'And God will wipe away every tear from their
eyes.'"

[8:1] *When he opened the seventh seal, there was silence in heaven for about half an hour.*

You will notice that today's passage is longer than the norm for this series. To read Revelation well, you and I will need to read each of the three sets of seven judgments (seals, trumpets, bowls) as a whole unit, which is why our passage is so long. But, too, we need to keep our eyes on what happens in heaven as well. John routinely interrupts these judgments with interludes, and today's passage has two of them, one in 7:1–8, and a second in 7:9–17. These interludes *teach us how to read the judgment*. In today's passage I have only bolded the words that teach us how to read the seven seals (6:9–11; 7:1–8; 7:9–17).

The seven seals are God's judgments on evil and injustice in this world *in response to the prayers of God's people and with the promise of final redemption for God's people*. The believers in the seven churches knew the hot breath of the dragon at work in Babylon, and they knew that some believers had been killed by Babylon, but they hear in these bolded words that Team Lamb will ultimately win, justice will be established, and New Jerusalem will replace Babylon. These words give these believers confidence, courage, and hope.

THE YEARNING OF GOD'S MARTYRS

Let's turn first to the bolded words, beginning with 6:9–11. The fifth seal, prayers of the martyrs, gives us a fresh perspective on the seven seals broken by the Lamb. John sees "under the altar the souls of those who had been slain because of the word of God and the testimony [=witness] they had maintained" (6:9). A witness, to repeat, is someone who has *seen* something about Jesus that the witness knows is true, and that person has the courage to *say* what they believe to be true, knowing that the consequence of seeing and saying is that they could *suffer* for it. Those under the altar are those whose suffering resulted in martyrdom.

121

Time has not worn them down. Eric Clapton, who with his guitar can turn emotion into music, once sang in his "Tears in Heaven," that . . .

Time can bring you down . . .
Have you begging please

Time surely wounds the believers on earth who long for justice, but those around the throne have the resilience characteristic only of God's empowering presence.

The martyrs for Jesus unite in a single prayer request that they send straight up to the One on the throne: "How long?" is their question, and their yearning is for God to "judge the inhabitants of the earth and avenge our blood" (6:10). I don't like the NIV's translation with the word "avenge" because it wreaks of vindictiveness and revenge. The term is the simple Greek term for "making things right." To make things right does not require God to torture and put to flames those who have acted unjustly. There is exposure of what has been done, admission of what has been done, and rectification of what was not done so that the people of God are no longer suffering. To put this in simple terms, there is far too much delight and even vindictiveness in too many who read this book and speculate about some future tribulation where all these seals are literally poured out over the earth.

God's response to their question and request is two-fold: (1) he gives them the white robe of purity because they are both in the right and asking for what is right, and (2) God informs them, and we get inside information, that they will need some patience (6:11). The perspective we gain by looking at these bolded words is that the seals are acts of God in making things right for the people of God in God's world.

On Reading the Seals, Trumpets, and Bowls

Many are disturbed and others deeply offended by the graphic depictions of judgment in Revelation 6–16. When John chose to write an "apocalypse" his entire book became apocalyptic. Apocalypses all contain scenes of cosmic disturbances at the hand of the divine. These judgments then are part of the genre.

The term "judgment" is too harsh, as if these seven times three actions are simply punitive. In fact, when one considers the tiny number of believers in western Asia Minor with the innumerable masses of believers by the end of these chapters, one must consider the seals, trumpets, and bowls as at least acts of divine discipline that provoke multitudes to turn their face and heart toward the Lamb.

Most important, these disciplines are unrealistic enough for us to think of them more in terms of a literary fiction, if not fantasy, than of predictions of what will occur on the human plane of reality. As Elizabeth Schüssler Fiorenza said, the Apocalypse is not "predictive-descriptive language but . . . mythological-imaginative language" and she added it "is mythological-fantastical language— stars fall from heaven . . . animals speak, dragons spit fire, a lion is a lamb, and angels or demons engage in warfare" (*Revelation*, 25).

So, look for exaggerations and symbols and

numbers to appear on the stage of Revelation, and be careful not to mistake exaggerations for realities.

Please read each discipline as a unit, even if the units are long and have interruptions in the flow. Those interruptions, or interludes, are designed to speak words of comfort to believers who are sensing Babylon's ugly grip. So, we will treat these sections as units: 6:1–8:1 (seals), 8:2–11:19 (trumpets), and then 15:1–16:21 (plagues of bowls).

The three times seven disciplines are a bitter sweetness for John in that he knows they are powerful acts and yet they will bring justice (10:1–11). They are answers to the prayers for justice by the suffering and oppressed people of God (6:9–11; 8:3–5), which means the people of God find these disciplines to be a just ending for them. Yet, the disciplines are not haphazard accidents in the world, but divine acts designed to bring justice and order to a world full of injustices. The Lamb bears responsibility for opening the seals, angels blow the trumpets, and all these in the presence of the One on the throne. These are acts of God, answers to the prayers of God's people, that end evil to bring in a world of peace (15:2–4; 16:4–7).

THE SEALING OF GOD'S PEOPLE

Revelation's seventh chapter describes four angels, to protect God's world and God's people, holding back the "four winds of the earth." Then another angel appears with the "seal of the living God" that will be used to mark, or seal, 144,000 persons from the "tribes of Israel" (7:1–4). Numbers, numbers, numbers. We must be careful. Seven means completion or even perfection, six means falling short of perfection, and 144,000 is 1,000 x 12 x 12, and points us to a complete number of Israelites—and New Jerusalem, as we will see, is a cube of 12,000 stadia with walls of 144 cubits. I'm with the many who think 144,000 represent the fullness of the *Jewish people of God who follow the Lamb*. And Brian Blount suggests that this is the "human wing of God's army" now fit for battle for the kingdom of God (Blount, *Revelation*, 145), but these 144,000 are believers in the Lamb as is clear in 14:1–5, in which passage they could be depicted like an ancient Israel military that does not have sex during wartime (cf. Deuteronomy 23:9–11; 2 Samuel 11:8–11). I have my doubts about this interpretation of the 144,000 and will explain it more at 14:1–5.

Following the 144,000, John widens his lens to see an innumerable host from "every nation, tribe, people and language" who are "standing before the throne and before the Lamb." Like the martyrs under the altar, they too wear white robes and wave in praise "palm branches" (7:9).

Instead of prayers, they open another ground of antiphonal praise to God and the Lamb (7:10–12): first, a choir of innumerable persons utterly interrupts the sixth seal from the seventh, to announce that "Salvation belongs to our God, who sits on the throne, and to the Lamb" (7:10). This, too, provides a powerful moment of release and courage for the small house churches in western Asia Minor. The angels, joined as they are by the 4+24, fall down and respond back to the host of believers with a Pentecostal-sounding "Amen!" and a listing of the attributes of God and the Lamb: praise, glory, wisdom, thanks, honor, power, and strength "be to our God for ever and ever." And they utter yet another "Amen!" Perhaps we should put a question mark instead of an exclamation point to see if they can get the innumerable host to sing again!

One of the twenty-four elders asks John, even though he knows, who the white robe folks are. John says, "you know," and then the elder informs John that these are those who have "come out of the great tribulation," who have "washed their robes" into whiteness "in the blood of the Lamb" (7:14). One can't of course wash robes white in blood, which serves to emphasize the symbolic character of the description. These wonderful saints are fit for the presence of God because of their witness and worship. In God's presence this innumerable host has risen into the throne room to "serve him day and night in his temple" where God will once again "shelter" them (7:15). The words stirred the first century listeners: they are promised that they will have food and drink, and they will be saved from the "scorching heat," a concern for anyone in the Mediterranean basin, and the Lamb himself will "shepherd them" as God wipes away all their pain and sorrow (7:15–17).

Please notice what happens when we hear the inside information of the prayers of the martyrs, that God seals 144,000, and that God will raise into his eternal presence those who suffered death at the hands of the dragon and the powers of Babylon. The rest of the seven seals need to be understood as divine discipline for the persecution of God's people while God protects those who have turned to the Lamb. While the judgments of these seals are graphic, the believers are looking for the good news that someday

God will make all things right. The seals are part of that divine right-making.

THE DISCIPLINES IN GOD'S WORLD

Now to the seals, and first we need to observe that there are some remarkable parallels between the seals, the trumpets, and the bowls.

	Seven Seals	Seven Trumpets	Seven Bowls
1.	White horse: war	Hail, fire, blood: 33%	Sores on humans
2.	Fire red horse: peace	Fiery mountain in sea: 33%	Blood in sea: death
3.	Black horse: famine	Wormwood star in rivers: 33%	Blood in rivers
4.	Pale horse: death	Sun, moon, stars, day: 33%	Sun scorches
5.	Martyrs praying	Woe #1: locusts unleashed	Beast's throne
6.	Cosmic signs	Woe #2: 33% of humans	River, frogs
7.	Silence	Woe #3: victory acclamation	Air: acclamation

Yet, the closest they get is the ending of each: silence that assumes the victories of the trumpets and bowls. That is, each of these divine disciplines lead straight to Babylon's fall, the elimination of evil, and the establishing of peace and justice. In this plot of justice, the seals provide general warnings about the plot of conquering, about the ending of peace in the world, about famine, and about the death of 25% of life on earth (6:1–8). Fearsome and gruesome. These are the four horses of the apocalypse, and they are horses sent out of Babylon. The machinations are orchestrated by the dragon.

The fifth seal, as we have seen, interrupts Babylon's march to rule the world with the prayers of the martyrs. As soon as those prayer requests are heard, John sees the sixth seal, which is about the Colossus Christ, the Lamb, whose judgments against the agents of the dragon and Babylon terrorize them (6:12–17). While many would read verse sixteen's fear and seventeen's question, "Who can withstand it?" as one of vengeance, I believe we can see in this a hint that at least some of Babylon's agents are coming to terms with the truth. What must never be missed in reading Revelation is the innumerableness of believers by the end of these disciplines. Perhaps the close of chapter six suggests that the Lamb will become their victor, too. Some battles lead to desertions and deserting the dragon's army is a victory for the Lamb.

What about the seventh seal? Nothing but silence, "for about half an hour" (8:1). The trumpets and bowls end, not with silence but the choirs singing "The kingdom of the world has become the kingdom of our Lord and his Messiah, and he will reign for ever and ever" (11:15) and "out of the temple came a loud voice from the throne" of God that utters "It is done!" or "It has happened" (16:17). The silence creates space for the acclamations of the Lamb's glorious victory over evil.

QUESTIONS FOR REFLECTION
AND APPLICATION

1. How is "witness" defined in this section?

2. How does God's presence empower Christians to be resilient, even in the face of martyrdom?

3. What is the difference between God avenging wrongs and God making things right?

4. In what ways is God's victory linked to overcoming injustice?

5. What prayers do you have for God's intervention in your life to make things right and just?

FOR FURTHER READING

Elizabeth Schüssler Fiorenza, *Revelation: Visions of a Just World* (Minneapolis: Fortress, 1992).

Eric Clapton, "Tears in Heaven." Source: Musixmatch Songwriters: Will Jennings / Eric Patrick Clapton Tears in Heaven lyrics © Blue Sky Rider Songs, E C Music Ltd.

THE BITTERSWEET
WITNESS

Revelation 8:2–11:19

*2 And I saw the seven angels who stand before God, and seven
trumpets were given to them. 3 Another angel, who had a golden
censer, came and stood at the altar. He was given much incense
to offer, with the prayers of all God's people, on the golden altar
in front of the throne. 4 The smoke of the incense, together with
the prayers of God's people, went up before God from the angel's
hand. 5 Then the angel took the censer, filled it with fire from the
altar, and hurled it on the earth; and there came peals of thunder, rumblings, flashes of lightning and an earthquake.*

*6 Then the seven angels who had the seven trumpets pre-
pared to sound them.*

*7 **The first angel sounded his trumpet,** and there came
hail and fire mixed with blood, and it was hurled down on the
earth. A third of the earth was burned up, a third of the trees
were burned up, and all the green grass was burned up.*

*8 **The second angel sounded his trumpet,** and something
like a huge mountain, all ablaze, was thrown into the sea. A
third of the sea turned into blood, 9 a third of the living creatures
in the sea died, and a third of the ships were destroyed.*

*10 **The third angel sounded his trumpet,** and a great star,* *blazing like a torch, fell from the sky on a third of the rivers and on the springs of water—[11] the name of the star is Wormwood. A third of the waters turned bitter, and many people died from the waters that had become bitter.*

[12] **The fourth angel sounded his trumpet,** *and a third of the sun was struck, a third of the moon, and a third of the stars, so that a third of them turned dark. A third of the day was without light, and also a third of the night.*

[13] *As I watched, I heard an eagle that was flying in midair call out in a loud voice: "Woe! Woe! Woe to the inhabitants of the earth, because of the trumpet blasts about to be sounded by the other three angels!"*

[9:1] **The fifth angel sounded his trumpet,** *and I saw a star that had fallen from the sky to the earth. The star was given the key to the shaft of the Abyss. [2] When he opened the Abyss, smoke rose from it like the smoke from a gigantic furnace. The sun and sky were darkened by the smoke from the Abyss. [3] And out of the smoke locusts came down on the earth and were given power like that of scorpions of the earth. [4] They were told not to harm the grass of the earth or any plant or tree, but only those people who did not have the seal of God on their foreheads. [5] They were not allowed to kill them but only to torture them for five months. And the agony they suffered was like that of the sting of a scorpion when it strikes. [6] During those days people will seek death but will not find it; they will long to die, but death will elude them.*

[7] *The locusts looked like horses prepared for battle. On their heads they wore something like crowns of gold, and their faces resembled human faces. [8] Their hair was like women's hair, and their teeth were like lions' teeth. [9] They had breastplates like breastplates of iron, and the sound of their wings was like the thundering of many horses and chariots rushing into battle. [10] They had tails with stingers, like scorpions, and in their tails*

they had power to torment people for five months. [11] *They had as king over them the angel of the Abyss, whose name in Hebrew is Abaddon and in Greek is Apollyon (that is, Destroyer).*

[12] *The first woe is past; two other woes are yet to come.*

[13] **The sixth angel sounded his trumpet,** *and I heard a voice coming from the four horns of the golden altar that is before God.* [14] *It said to the sixth angel who had the trumpet, "Release the four angels who are bound at the great river Euphrates."* [15] *And the four angels who had been kept ready for this very hour and day and month and year were released to kill a third of mankind.* [16] *The number of the mounted troops was twice ten thousand times ten thousand. I heard their number.*

[17] *The horses and riders I saw in my vision looked like this: Their breastplates were fiery red, dark blue, and yellow as sulfur. The heads of the horses resembled the heads of lions, and out of their mouths came fire, smoke and sulfur.* [18] *A third of mankind was killed by the three plagues of fire, smoke and sulfur that came out of their mouths.* [19] *The power of the horses was in their mouths and in their tails; for their tails were like snakes, having heads with which they inflict injury.*

[20] *The rest of mankind who were not killed by these plagues still did not repent of the work of their hands; they did not stop worshiping demons, and idols of gold, silver, bronze, stone and wood—idols that cannot see or hear or walk.* [21] *Nor did they repent of their murders, their magic arts, their sexual immorality or their thefts.*

[10:1] **Then I saw another mighty angel coming down from heaven. He was robed in a cloud, with a rainbow above his head; his face was like the sun, and his legs were like fiery pillars.** [2] **He was holding a little scroll, which lay open in his hand. He planted his right foot on the sea and his left foot on the land,** [3] **and he gave a loud shout like the roar of a lion. When he shouted, the voices of the seven thunders** spoke. *4 And when the seven thunders spoke, I was about to write; but I heard a voice from heaven say, "Seal up what the seven thunders have said and do not write it down."*

5 Then the angel I had seen standing on the sea and on the land raised his right hand to heaven. 6 And he swore by him who lives for ever and ever, who created the heavens and all that is in them, the earth and all that is in it, and the sea and all that is in it, and said, "There will be no more delay! 7 But in the days when the seventh angel is about to sound his trumpet, the mystery of God will be accomplished, just as he announced to his servants the prophets."

8 Then the voice that I had heard from heaven spoke to me once more: "Go, take the scroll that lies open in the hand of the angel who is standing on the sea and on the land."

9 So I went to the angel and asked him to give me the little scroll. He said to me, "Take it and eat it. It will turn your stomach sour, but 'in your mouth it will be as sweet as honey.'" 10 I took the little scroll from the angel's hand and ate it. It tasted as sweet as honey in my mouth, but when I had eaten it, my stomach turned sour. 11 Then I was told, "You must prophesy again about many peoples, nations, languages and kings."

11:1 I was given a reed like a measuring rod and was told, "Go and measure the temple of God and the altar, with its worshipers. 2 But exclude the outer court; do not measure it, because it has been given to the Gentiles. They will trample on the holy city for 42 months. 3 And I will appoint my two witnesses, and they will prophesy for 1,260 days, clothed in sackcloth." 4 They are "the two olive trees" and the two lampstands, and "they stand before the Lord of the earth." 5 If anyone tries to harm them, fire comes from their mouths and devours their enemies. This is how any-one who wants to harm them must die. ⁶ *They have power to shut up the heavens so that it will not rain during the time they are prophesying; and they have power to turn the waters into blood and to strike the earth with every kind of plague as often as they want.*

⁷ *Now when they have finished their testimony, the beast that comes up from the Abyss will attack them, and overpower and kill them.* ⁸ *Their bodies will lie in the public square of the great city—which is figuratively called Sodom and Egypt—where also their Lord was crucified.* ⁹ *For three and a half days some from every people, tribe, language and nation will gaze on their bodies and refuse them burial.* ¹⁰ *The inhabitants of the earth will gloat over them and will celebrate by sending each other gifts, be-cause these two prophets had tormented those who live on the earth.*

¹¹ *But after the three and a half days the breath of life from God entered them, and they stood on their feet, and terror struck those who saw them.* ¹² *Then they heard a loud voice from heaven saying to them, "Come up here." And they went up to heaven in a cloud, while their enemies looked on.*

¹³ *At that very hour there was a severe earthquake and a tenth of the city collapsed. Seven thousand people were killed in the earthquake, and the survivors were terrified and gave glory to the God of heaven.*

¹⁴ *The second woe has passed; the third woe is coming soon.*

¹⁵ The seventh angel sounded his trumpet, *and there were loud voices in heaven, which said:*

"*The kingdom of the world has become*

> the kingdom of our Lord and of his Messiah,
> and he will reign for ever and ever."

¹⁶ And the twenty-four elders, who were seated on their thrones before God, fell on their faces and worshiped God, ¹⁷ saying:

> "We give thanks to you, Lord God Almighty,
>   the One who is and who was,
> because you have taken your great power
>   and have begun to reign.
> ¹⁸ The nations were angry,
>   and your wrath has come.
> The time has come for judging the dead,
>   and for rewarding your servants the prophets
> and your people who revere your name,
>   both great and small—
> and for destroying those who destroy the earth."

¹⁹ Then God's temple in heaven was opened, and within his temple was seen the ark of his covenant. And there came flashes of lightning, rumblings, peals of thunder, an earthquake and a severe hailstorm.

Today's passage begins with silence that prompts the "prayers of all God's people" (8:3). These are the intercessions of the people of God, Team Lamb, for justice and peace (cf. 6:10). The divine disciplines are answers to the prayers of God's people to end injustice and oppression and to establish justice and peace. Think of the suffering people of Ukraine who pray daily for the end of Putin's war against Ukraine. Think of the families in the USA whose children have been shot in the safety of their schools. Think of the systemic racism that prevents progress for African, Latin, and Asian Americans. These are the ones represented by the angel with the "golden censer" (8:3). These are the ones who want their prayers answered and find courage and hope when that great angel tosses those prayers from the throne room onto the earth. Those prayers lead to the seven trumpets. The seven trumpets are not vengeance but God letting justice roll.

As with the seals so with the seven trumpets, we will look at the whole unit rather than break it into separate paragraphs. And again, the bolded words are interludes interrupting the flow of John's description of the seven trumpets. The interludes suspend the listeners between the sixth and the seventh, providing relief and hope and perspective on the disciplines at work in the seven trumpets. So, again, we begin with the words in bold.

BITTERSWEET SCROLL

To be called onto a Christian platform to preach may look like glory but, believe me, at times it's a burden hard to tote. When I was traveling all over speaking about the *Jesus Creed*, it was only the nerves of a new audience and wondering if they'd embrace me as their speaker that day. But when I wrote *Revelation for the Rest of Us*, I knew the days of "Thanks, Scot, I got a lot out of that" were over. Once, after I spoke on a difficult topic, a man came straight up to me, looked me in the eyes, and said, "The devil told more truth in the Garden of Eden than you told in your sermon this evening."

I am but an agent for John speaking about *his* apocalypse, not mine. But I felt and feel a burden to challenge American churches for their complicity in Babylon. It means talking about politics, and Washington, D.C., and presidents and candidates for office in the nation, at the state level, and in various local contexts. It's a lot easier to talk about love to various audiences than to challenge political corruption and church complicity on the basis of Revelation 17–19!

John sees yet "another mighty angel," glorious in appearance, who has a little scroll opened in his hand. He lands on earth with the right foot "on the sea" and the other "on the land." (This anticipates chapter thirteen.) His shout sounds like a lion's roar, which elicits the antiphony of the "voices of the seven thunders," who evidently want to toss more divine judgment on the earth . . . but God interrupts and tells the thunders to close up shop and go home. Never to be heard from again.

The mighty angel with feet on land and sea declares that the time is about up because the seventh trumpet is about to blow (11:15–19). When that final trumpet is heard "the mystery of God will be accomplished" (10:7). Frankly, the word "mystery" leaves us hanging, but wait for it, 11:15 reveals what that mystery is: "The kingdom of the world has become the kingdom of our Lord and of his Messiah, and he will reign for ever and ever" (11:15). The End. The New Jerusalem. So, the seventh trumpet will take us straight to the end of the book of Revelation. But we're not there yet.

The "voice" orders John to grab the scroll from the straddling angel. This echoes Revelation 5, until we get to what John hears next. He's told not that he gets to break the seals, but, like Ezekiel 2:9–3:3, to "eat it," with the important nutrition label that reads, "It will turn your stomach sour, but 'in your mouth it will be as sweet as honey.'" He eats it as told, and what was told happened. He got a sour stomach. All which leads to the burden of his calling as an apocalyptist: "You must prophesy again about many peoples, nations, languages and kings" (10:9–11).

Notice again those last lines. John is not just witnessing to western Asia Minor believers in those seven churches. His witness extends to and is about the whole world. This theme of the gospel going to the whole world alone explains how so many humans end up worshiping the Lamb in Revelation (cf. 5:9; 7:9; 11:9). In Revelation 14:6 evangelism of the whole world is explicit—an angel "had the eternal gospel to proclaim to those who live on the earth—to every nation, tribe, language and people."

What the listeners hear is that what John is about to unveil is a bittersweet calling: it can taste ever so sweet at times, but it sours the stomach. The seven seals, trumpets, ignoring the thunders, and bowls both indicate judgment is coming, but what happens is a bittersweet experience for all humans. No one should enjoy these judgments; no one should gloat in some kind of triumphalism; no one should say *Glad I won't experience that*. Instead, we should read them and grieve over the condition of humans who have been imprisoned in Babylon by the dragon and his wild things.

BITTERSWEET WITNESSES

We all ask. So let's start with, who are these two witnesses? Guessing comes easy. Too easy. Ian Paul makes a case for these two witnesses being "a metaphorical description of the people of God" (Paul, *Revelation*, 198). I'm not so sure that we can expand the two to all the people of God. These witnesses, like the end of chapter seven's innumerable host (7:14), are martyrs. The "beast that comes up from the

Abyss" kills them (11:7). In gruesome language, the bodies of the two witnesses "lie in the public square of the great city" for three and a half days (11:8; Jerusalem is the city). Surprisingly the "inhabitants of the earth will gloat over" these rotting bodies (11:10). Backing up to the beginning of the chapter's description of a temple that reminds of Ezekiel 40–42, we learn "Gentiles . . . will trample on the holy city for 42 months," that is, three-and-a-half years (11:2). The two witnesses proclaim the Lamb in the midst of gentile opposition inspired by the beast from the abyss. During that time the two witnesses exercise extraordinary powers over life and death and the weather (11:3–6). Like Lazarus and the saints of Jerusalem, they are raised from the dead and ascend to the throne (11:11–12), following which an earthquake devastates Jerusalem, killing 7,000 but turning others to God (11:13).

One hears an echo of Zechariah 3–4 and 6:9–14, that is, the priestly and Davidic messiahs, in these two witnesses when one hears the words about the "two olive trees" (Revelation 11:4). Like Moses and Elijah, they administer plagues. And two witnesses confirm the truth of what is said (Deuteronomy 19:15). I side with those who see these two witnesses representing those who have witnessed to the Lamb and been martyred for it. Yet, one could understand the two witnesses as representatives of all those on Team Lamb.

If we read, as we should, chapters ten and eleven together, something rushes to the front: during these divine disciplines of seven trumpets, the call of the people of God is to witness to the Lamb. But *their witness will be a bittersweet reality.* Jesus' followers will stand up and speak out, and they will also experience opposition, at times leading to martyrdom. Instead of gloating over the defeat of

Team Dragon—the kind of gloating seen in Team Dragon in 11:10—believers are called to be witnesses because the disciplines of God will lead some to give "glory to the God of heaven" (11:12), and they will join the innumerable host of believers in New Jerusalem.

To read Revelation with a deep resonance requires that we long, desire, and ache for justice in this world. That we long for the oppressed to be liberated. That war and corruption be turned into peace and righteousness. If we are reading the book to find out what's gonna happen so we can guess who today is doing what in the book of Revelation, we fail this book. Today's long passage, again, begins with prayers for justice. That's the spirit and mood of those who need to listen to the promise of God to bring about justice and peace. Those who love New Jerusalem have the eyes of wisdom to discern the reality of the dragon and his Babylon.

Babylon Today: Gun Culture's Idolatry

A mark of ancient Rome and Babylon was its murderous ways. The threat of death and public deaths, Babylon knows, cowers people into submission. Death threats lead to domination.

Guns are designed to kill.

Today there are about 393 million privately owned firearms in the United States, according to an estimate by the Switzerland-based Small Arms Survey—in other words, 120 guns for every 100 Americans. That's the highest rate of any country in the world, and more than double that of the next country on the list (Emba).

The Centers for Disease Control and Prevention recorded 48,830 U.S. firearm deaths in 2021, the last year for which complete data is available. Those include suicides—which have long accounted for the majority of US gun deaths—as well as homicides (NPR1).

In the United States, there were more than 200 mass shootings in 2023 before the year was even half over, according to the Gun Violence Archive. The nonprofit defines a mass shooting as an incident where at least four people are killed or injured. In recent years, these shootings have occurred in places of worship, medical offices, elementary schools, and outdoor events. Knowing how to react in an active shooting is now necessary, according to Alex del Carmen, associate dean and professor of criminology at Tarleton State University. "Many Americans are going to experience this at some point in their lives," del Carmen told NPR in a phone interview. "We now have almost an obligation to teach children and family members what to do in these situations." Del Carmen has told his kids since they were little: Have an exit plan (NPR 2).

Perhaps the most troubling aspect of gun ownership for "protection" is the sharp-edged individualism it implies: an every-man-for-himself mindset. Institutions can't be trusted, police will be unresponsive, and the government might one day turn on you. Your only obligations are to yourself and your family.

Individual fear becomes a greater priority than collective safety. Increasing the number of guns in the system will almost certainly spell death for others, but at least *your* gun will keep *you* safe (Emba).

Over and over again, I heard the NRA-approved phrase: "An armed society is a polite society." But guns might be leading us to give up on the concept of society altogether (Emba).

James Atwood, who has probably thought about gun control as much, if not more, than any American alive today has reflected on idolatry of guns, and he has shown that the American commitment to guns approaches and crosses the line of idolatry. To own a gun is to have ultimate power; the desire for ultimate power is a desire to usurp God's providence. Atwood perceives gun idolatry in the following three elements:

1. When an owner [of a gun] believes there are no circumstances when a regulation or restriction for public safety should be placed upon it [the gun/the owner].
2. When an owner believes that guns don't kill; they only save lives.
3. When an owner has no doubt that guns preserve America's most cherished values.

Atwood advises looking for deep emotional attachment to guns, anger when anyone questions gun values, when no preventive measures are supported, show little to no grief for those who have experienced gun violence, vigorously oppose any restrictions of sales of guns, claim an absolute right to use their guns against the government if they consider it tyrannical, claim the blessing of God on the weapon, and believe the solution to gun violence is more guns (McKnight).

THE TRUMPETS AND THEIR WOES

John surrounds his record of the seven trumpets with the calling to be a bittersweet witness. Noticeably, if the seven seals had a more general feel for distress in the world, the seven trumpets have a partial feel. This is seen in two ways: 33% judgments and a five-month judgment. This partial feel reveals that God sends these judgments so humans will end their injustices and turn in repentance to become witnesses and worshipers of the Lamb. The fictions and fantasies of the apocalyptic move in these seven trumpets into graphic destruction.

First Trumpet: hail, fire, blood; 33% of the earth and trees and all grass burns.

Second Trumpet: fiery mountain tossed into sea; 33% of sea turns into blood, 33% of sea creatures die, 33% of ships destroyed.

Third Trumpet: a great, fiery star named "Wormwood" falls into 33% of rivers and sources of water, 33% of waters are bitter and "many people" die.

Fourth Trumpet: 33% of sun, moon, and stars struck with darkness; 33% of day and night struck.

Trumpets five, six, and seven escalate the answers to prayers, leading these trumpets also to be labeled as "woes."

Fifth Trumpet/first Woe: a star falls to the earth with a key to the "abyss," which the star opens. Smoke from a burning furnace is released as the doom of darkness. Out of the abyss arises locusts who torment *for only five months* those who do "not have the seal of God on their foreheads." The locusts, described in image-busting detail, are agents of Abbadon or Apollyon, Hebrew and Greek terms for "Destroyer" (9:7–11).

Sixth Trumpet/second Woe: a voice from the "four horns of the golden altar that is before God" orders the sixth angel to release the four angels "bound at the great river Euphrates." An almost innumerable army of horse-mounted warriors are released to "kill a third of mankind" with "fire, smoke and sulfur" (9:15, 17).

The disciplinary nature of these gruesome, graphic acts permitted by God must be seen for what they are: answers to prayer for justice and acts of God to persuade people to turn from their injustices and oppressions. That is, to come out of Babylon with its allegiances to the dragon and turn to God. An innumerable host will turn but not all. Sadly, Revelation 9:20–21 reveals that many resist the disciplines of God and refuse to repent of their idolatries, murders, "magic arts," immoralities, and thefts. These resistances not only reveal that humans are agents with choice but that the acts are designed by God to open their eyes to injustices. Since I read Revelation as apocalyptic, and thus full of fiction and fantasy and imagery, I don't think it is at all helpful to read these images as literal realities on planet earth. They are designed to provoke the imagination of the people of God and all those who will listen. A provoked imagination leads to a person reconsidering their place before God and their relations with others in this world, and to probe their inner heart to see if it is committed to justice or injustice, to peace or oppression.

At this point John inserts the bittersweet scenes about the scroll, the temple, gentile persecution of the people of God, and the two witnesses. Only then does John turn finally to the last trumpet.

Seventh Trumpet/third Woe: Unlike the previous six trumpets and the previous two Woes, the seventh trumpet pulls back the curtains for us to see not an act of discipline but a choir of voices singing or chanting in heaven the words of God's victory over sin and Satan and systemic injustices (11:15–19). The songs again are antiphonal: the "voices" say "the kingdom of the world has become the kingdom of our Lord and his Messiah." The twenty-four elders then fall down and worship God with words or thanks for assuming divine power (11:17), for judging evil and "rewarding your servants the prophets," and for "destroying those who destroy the earth" (11:18). That last expression, "those who destroy the earth," both takes us back to the acts of destruction in the first four seals (6:1–8) and it makes us, or at least me, wonder if the six trumpets were not imagery for the dragon using humans on earth to destroy. Those who follow the Lamb not only are bittersweet witnesses, but they join the heavenly choirs as bittersweet dissidents of the way of Babylon.

The seven trumpets end with a scene in heaven. God's temple is opened so all of us can see the "ark of his covenant," the covenant that promises blessings for those who follow the way of the Lamb. Once we see that ark, we hear the powers of the cosmos shaking (11:19), all signs of things to come.

146

QUESTIONS FOR REFLECTION
AND APPLICATION

1. What is the significance of the trumpets of God's justice for those praying and interceding?

2. How does John's apocalypse start with messages to one region but branch out to become a message to the whole world?

3. What should our disposition be toward the coming judgment and discipline? Gloating, sorrow, something else?

4. In what ways have you seen humans doing the destructive work of the dragon on earth?

5. How do you feel when you need to speak difficult messages from the Bible that your audience might not like? How can John's example help you?

FOR FURTHER READING

Christine Emba, https://www.washingtonpost.com
/opinions/2023/05/15/gun-show-customers
-fear-society/.

McKnight: https://scotmcknight.substack.com/p
/following-jesus-without-the-second.

NPR1: https://www.npr.org/2023/05/12
/1173141518/gun-violence-prevention-public
-health.

NPR2: https://www.npr.org/2023/05/09
/1174944649/safety-tips-mass-shooting-run
-hide-fight.

THE WOMAN AND THE DRAGON

Revelation 12:1–17

[1] *A great sign appeared in heaven: a woman clothed with the sun, with the moon under her feet and a crown of twelve stars on her head.* [2] *She was pregnant and cried out in pain as she was about to give birth.* [3] *Then another sign appeared in heaven: an enormous red dragon with seven heads and ten horns and seven crowns on its heads.* [4] *Its tail swept a third of the stars out of the sky and flung them to the earth. The dragon stood in front of the woman who was about to give birth, so that it might devour her child the moment he was born.* [5] *She gave birth to a son, a male child, who "will rule all the nations with an iron scepter." And her child was snatched up to God and to his throne.* [6] *The woman fled into the wilderness to a place prepared for her by God, where she might be taken care of for 1,260 days.*

[7] *Then war broke out in heaven. Michael and his angels fought against the dragon, and the dragon and his angels fought back.* [8] *But he was not strong enough, and they lost their place in heaven.* [9] *The great dragon was hurled down—that ancient serpent called the devil, or Satan, who leads the whole world astray. He was hurled to the earth, and his angels with him.*

¹⁰ *Then I heard a loud voice in heaven say:*

> *"Now have come the salvation and the power*
> *and the kingdom of our God,*
> *and the authority of his Messiah.*
> *For the accuser of our brothers and sisters,*
> *who accuses them before our God day and night,*
> *has been hurled down.*
> ¹¹ *They triumphed over him*
> *by the blood of the Lamb*
> *and by the word of their testimony;*
> *they did not love their lives so much*
> *as to shrink from death.*
> ¹² *Therefore rejoice, you heavens*
> *and you who dwell in them!*
> *But woe to the earth and the sea,*
> *because the devil has gone down to you!*
> *He is filled with fury,*
> *because he knows that his time is short."*

¹³ *When the dragon saw that he had been hurled to the earth, he pursued the woman who had given birth to the male child.* ¹⁴ *The woman was given the two wings of a great eagle, so that she might fly to the place prepared for her in the wilderness, where she would be taken care of for a time, times and half a time, out of the serpent's reach.* ¹⁵ *Then from his mouth the serpent spewed water like a river, to overtake the woman and sweep her away with the torrent.* ¹⁶ *But the earth helped the woman by opening its mouth and swallowing the river that the dragon had spewed out of his mouth.* ¹⁷ *Then the dragon was enraged at the woman and went off to wage war against the rest of her offspring—those who keep God's commands and hold fast their testimony about Jesus.*

On Patmos and in heaven John saw two women—Roma, the goddess of Rome depicted as the whore of Babylon in Revelation 17–19, and a woman in Revelation 12 who seems to morph from one woman into two others. Speaking of morphing, as the Lion morphs into the Lamb in chapter five, so in Revelation 12 the dragon morphs in today's passage.

To read Revelation 12 well we need both a good imagination and to back up to Genesis 3. In Genesis 3, the serpent tricks the woman into eating the fruit on the tree of the knowledge of good and evil. Thinking her eyes might be opened, she enters into a world of sin and corruption and deception. Here are the words of the Lord God to the serpent and to Eve and to Adam, words that shape one way to read the history of the world:

> So the LORD God said to the serpent, "Because you have done this . . .
>
>> I will put enmity
>>> between you and the woman,
>>> and between your offspring and hers;
>> he will crush your head,
>>> and you will strike his heel." (Genesis 3:14–15)

The cosmic struggle, our cosmic struggle, entered into human history from Eden on until . . . yes, until Jesus who conquered Satan and until New Jerusalem when Satan will be finally and forever banished from corrupting the children of Eve. Notice these features of this cosmic story: the serpent is alive and well; the serpent opposes the woman; the serpent's days are numbered, and its doom is sure. Most important, God reveals to the serpent that the seed of the woman "will crush your head" even though "you will strike his heel" (3:15). In the Bible's narrative the striking of the heel was the crucifixion of Jesus and the crushing of the head pertains to the resurrection, the ascension, and the return of Jesus as King of kings and Lord of lords. Revelation 17–19 and 20–22 are the final answer to Genesis 3:15.

Revelation 12 is not what happens next in some chronological order. Revelation 12 is a vision of the whole sweep of Revelation. Today's chapter is the story of everything. If you want to reduce Revelation to its basics, you can't do much better than Revelation 12. The Christian is called in this chapter to conquer evil in this world "by the blood of the Lamb and the by the word of their testimony." That is, by signing up for Team Lamb, for witnessing to the Lamb, and for joining in with the heavenly choirs to sing the song of the dragon's dissidents in 12:10–12.

A MORPHING WOMAN

John sees a "great sign" in heaven. The sign beckons us to listen carefully and to imagine in our minds what John describes. Three moments in this chapter suggest that this woman morphs. First, she sounds like Israel (12:1). A woman "clothed with the sun with the moon under her feet and a crown of twelve stars on her head," when we know the woman of Babylon stands for Rome, sounds like Israel in Jerusalem. Second, she "was pregnant and cried out in pain as she was about to give birth" (12:2; cf. Isaiah 66:7–9; Micah 4:8–10). This sounds like Mary, mother of Jesus. In fact, she is, because 12:5 explicitly tells us this woman gives birth to "a son, a male child, who 'will rule the nations'" and her son "was snatched up to God and to his throne." That's the resurrection and ascension of Jesus. But third, she sounds like the church when we get to 12:13–17 because the woman's offspring refers to those who "keep God's commands and hold fast to their testimony about Jesus." Some prefer to see the woman as nothing more than the people of God. I prefer to see her morphing from Israel to Mary to the church. Yes, on the whole, the people of God, but the sharpness of the descriptions suggest a more nuanced profile can be gleaned.

A MORPHING DRAGON

No sooner has John described the woman in 12:1–2 than we meet up with "another sign" that is "an enormous red dragon." This red dragon sounds almost like the woman of Babylon because the dragon has "seven heads and ten horns and seven crowns on its head" (see too Daniel 7:2–7). Powers sweep 33% of the stars (Daniel 8:10) onto the earth (sounds like the first five trumpets). Destruction describes the dragon (cf. 9:11). Dragons appear in the Bible (Job 26:13; Psalms 74:13–14; 104:26).

This dragon morphs in chapter twelve from dragon to serpent, and the serpent is named as the devil or Satan (12:3, 9, 14). Jeremiah connects serpent with the king of Babylon (51:34).

What the dragon most wants is to devour the woman's male-child. That sounds like Genesis 3:15's description of the serpent striking the heel of the woman's seed. But the dragon fails because God "raptures" (yes, that's the word in Revelation 12:5) the son to the throne room where the Son will morph into the Lion and the Lamb. To escape, the woman "fled into the wilderness" where she would be protected for a time, and that time yet again is three-and-a-half years. This number in Revelation indicates "for awhile" or "for a short period."

The Dragon and Python

Many think John's story of the dragon and the woman evokes a Latin story about Python, Leto, and Apollo. It's at least suggestive.

It has clear connections to a myth that was widely circulated from the third century BC to the second century AD in a variety of forms, the best known being the story of Leto, Python, and Apollo. Python, a huge dragon, was warned by an oracle that he would be destroyed by one of Leto's children. Leto was a lover of Zeus who was married to Hera. When Hera learned that Leto was pregnant, she banished her; Leto gave birth to her twins, Artemis and Apollo, on the island of Delos [near Patmos]. Python pursued her in order to destroy her offspring, but she was carried away by Aquilo (Latin for the north wind) and protected by Poseidon with waves. When four days old, Apollo hunted down Python and killed him with arrows (both Apollo and Artemis were archers). This story was used as imperial propaganda, particularly by Domitian, to portray the emperor as Apollo, the son of the gods, and defeater of the chaos monster.

From Ian Paul, *Revelation*, 214.

WOMAN VS. DRAGON IS COSMIC

Jesus prayed for God's will to be done on earth as it was in heaven (Matthew 6:10), but in Revelation's twelfth chapter we find that God's will in heaven has its challengers! So much so a "war broke out in heaven" (12:7) between Team Lamb's heavenly cohort—Michael and his angels—and Team Dragon and its heavenly cohort. Michael wins and tosses the dragon to earth. At this point the dragon morphs into the "ancient serpent" (from Genesis 3) who is called "the devil, or Satan" (12:9).

A cosmic song of praise erupts in the courts of the throne room that calls on the heavens to "rejoice" but the earth to be warned of coming destruction and death at the hand of the dragon and its cohort of demons. Their song, which again is the song of dissidents who resist in song, announces (1) that redemption has come through the Lamb, (2) that the witnesses of the Lamb have conquered in spite of their martyrdom, (3) that the heavens should rejoice, and (4) that the earth is in for a time of trouble (12:10–12).

As in heaven, so on earth. The dragon now pursues the woman and her offspring. Again, John tells us in more detail that the woman escaped into the wilderness to be protected for a short period. The dragon's first method of attack is to spew water out of his mouth like a gushing river. But God's good earth absorbs the water. Realizing God's got the woman covered, the dragon goes after the "rest of her offspring," some of whom he will nab and kill. But the witness of the Lamb's followers will conquer because the Lamb has himself defeated death and the dragon.

One more time: Revelation 12 puts into one set of

morphing images the entire story of Revelation. It is the story of sin and salvation, death and destruction, all played on a cosmic stage with the main actors being the woman and the dragon. If you want to teach your children or a youth group the book of Revelation, start with today's passage, master the imagery, and read the whole book as a battle between good and evil, justice and injustice, truth and the lie, the woman and the dragon, and between the people of God and the dragon and its cohort. That's all one needs to know to get this book right.

QUESTIONS FOR REFLECTION AND APPLICATION

1. How does Revelation 12 function as a summary of the whole book?

2. What connections does this section have to Old Testament passages?

3. How might the woman represent Israel, Mary, and the church?

4. In this passage, which elements inspire hope in you?

5. What do you want to thank God for in light of this passage?

THE DRAGON'S BEASTS OF CONFORMITY

Revelation 13:1–18

[1] The **dragon** stood on the shore of the sea. And I saw **a beast coming out of the sea**. It had ten horns and seven heads, with ten crowns on its horns, and on each head a blasphemous name. [2] The beast I saw resembled a leopard, but had feet like those of a bear and a mouth like that of a lion. The **dragon** gave the beast his power and his throne and great authority. [3] One of the heads of the beast seemed to have had a fatal wound, but the fatal wound had been healed. The whole world was filled with wonder and followed the beast. [4] People worshiped the **dragon** because he had given authority to the beast, and they also worshiped the beast and asked, "Who is like the beast? Who can wage war against it?"

[5] The beast was given a mouth to utter proud words and blasphemies and to exercise its authority for forty-two months. [6] It opened its mouth to blaspheme God, and to slander his name and his dwelling place and those who live in heaven. [7] It was given power to wage war against God's holy people and to conquer them. And it was given authority over every tribe, people,

language and nation. [8] All inhabitants of the earth will worship the beast—all whose names have not been written in the Lamb's book of life, the Lamb who was slain from the creation of the world.

[9] Whoever has ears, let them hear.

> [10] "If anyone is to go into captivity,
> into captivity they will go.
> If anyone is to be killed with the sword,
> with the sword they will be killed."

This calls for patient endurance and faithfulness on the part of God's people.

[11] Then I saw **a second beast, coming out of the earth.** It had two horns like a lamb, but it spoke like a **dragon.** [12] It exercised all the authority of the first beast on its behalf, and made the earth and its inhabitants worship the first beast, whose fatal wound had been healed. [13] And it performed great signs, even causing fire to come down from heaven to the earth in full view of the people. [14] Because of the signs it was given power to perform on behalf of the first beast, it deceived the inhabitants of the earth. It ordered them to set up an image in honor of the beast who was wounded by the sword and yet lived. [15] The second beast was given power to give breath to the image of the first beast, so that the image could speak and cause all who refused to worship the image to be killed. [16] It also forced all people, great and small, rich and poor, free and slave, to receive a mark on their right hands or on their foreheads, [17] so that they could not buy or sell unless they had the mark, which is the name of the beast or the number of its name. [18] This calls for wisdom. Let the person who has insight calculate the number of the beast, for it is the number of a man. That number is 666.

The dragon's battle against God—the woman, her son, her offspring—requires agents to do the dragon's dirty work. That is, the cosmic battle requires earthly, human agents who will carry out the mission of the dragon, who again is Satan (12:9). Followers of the Lamb need "wisdom" (13:18) to discern the agents, that is, to discern the deceivers from the truth-tellers. As the Lord has appointed two witnesses (11:1–14), so the ultimate copy-cat, Satan, finds two beasts to accomplish the mission of death and destruction. Even more, Revelation 11:7 revealed a "beast that comes up from the Abyss" who killed the two witnesses. Revelation 13, no doubt, explains that sudden mention of a beast.

Many are driven to speculate about who today (Putin?) is doing what in the book of Revelation. Such a reading treats the book as needing a decoder. The Apocalypse is for ordinary believers in small house churches in western Asia Minor. Its purpose is not to stimulate speculation but instead to stimulate witness for the Lamb and worship of the Lamb, all with a capacity of wisdom to discern the realities of Babylon. Today's passage teaches us to nurture the wisdom to discern the work of the dragon in the powers of our day, that is, in the beasts alive and well now. Babylon is timeless; the beasts are timeless. All because the dragon is timeless, until his doom, when both Babylon and the beasts will disappear with the dragon.

Babylon Today: What Is Empire?

Michael Gorman defines empire today in the following words:

> An entity that has come to widespread global or nearly global dominance through deliberate expansion by means of the extreme exercise of some forms of power—economic, political, military, and or religious—resulting in the creation of colony-like clients of the entity and of enemies who perceive the entity as oppressive.

> Michael Gorman, *Reading Revelation Responsibly* (Eugene, OR: Cascade Books, 2011, p. 45, all in italics in original).

WISDOM TO DISCERN THE PRESENCE OF ANTICHRISTS

The book of Revelation never mentions *the* Antichrist, though nearly everyone who speculates about the final Antichrist believes the beast, or beasts, are that Antichrist. Yes and No. In the early churches, four different figures arise to such a similar level of evil and dominance: the "false christs" mentioned by Jesus (Mark 13:22), the "man of lawlessness" (2 Thessalonians 2:3, 7–9), the many antichrists of 1 John (2:18, 22; 4:3; 2 John 7), and the two beasts of Revelation 13, one of whom is embodied in the "666" name (13:18). Notice that only one time is such a figure reduced to one person, while if the author of Revelation is the author of 1 John, John thinks there is not one but many. As Babylon is timeless, so also are antichrists always available to serve the dragon. So, yes, the beasts are antichrists, but they are not one, final Antichrist. In looking for one Antichrist, many fail to see a number of antichrists in the world. In speculating about one predicted Antichrist—Hitler? Stalin? Putin?—the speculators fail to acquire the wisdom to discern the presence of antichrists in our nation and in our own backyards. Who cannot see an antichrist in North Korea's Kim Jong Un? Or in the religious coercions toward conformity in cults? Or in bosses and parents and pastors who demand total allegiance?

The term *anti*christ, or *anti*-Messiah, reveals their mission. To oppose and thwart the Messiah or Lamb and the Lamb's followers. The antichrists' mission, like that of the dragon, is to kill and consume the Messiah, the woman, and the offspring of the woman (12:17). For our sake we must adjust our thinking to John's thinking: *there are always antichrists working for the dragon in our world, and our calling is to discern their presence and recognize their corruptions.* Wherever it may be found.

WISDOM TO DISCERN AGENTS OF THE DRAGON

The dragon opposes the Lamb. Team Dragon forms into the institution he calls Babylon. The marks of Babylon are the way of the dragon to work its mission of deception, destruction, and death. What jumps out from Revelation 13 is that two beasts are agents of the dragon, that is, agents of Babylon. In fact, beast #2 (from the "earth" or "land") is a sycophantic agent of the beast #1 (from the "sea"). So here's the hierarchy of Team Dragon:

Dragon
    Babylon
        Beast #1
            Beast #2

Babylon turns the way of the dragon into a system, an institution, a city. The Beasts merely carry out the system established by the dragon. The marks of Babylon become behaviors through Agent Beast of the sea and Agent Beast of the earth. If we are discerning disciples, we will see in leaders in our world the marks of Babylon and so perceive the agents of the dragon.

In today's text, notice the word "dragon" (in bold above) appearing four times. But notice even more:

1. The dragon seems to call forth the beast from the sea (13:1).
2. The "dragon gave the beast his power and his throne and great authority" (13:2).
3. The "people worshiped the dragon" because it empowered the beast (13:4).
4. The people also worshiped the beast (13:4).
5. The second beast "spoke like a dragon" (13:11).

Babylon and the beasts are agents of the dragon, and in their work, we are called to have the wisdom to see the work of the dragon.

The marks of Babylon are all over the beasts in today's passage: blasphemous idolatries, power and authority and a throne, murderous treatment of the people of the

Lamb, death and destruction, the pervasive presence of images that are to be worshiped, and a world-wide reach of empire. So dominant are the beasts that they mark people with a sign that makes them fit for Babylon and all others cannot trade in merchandise or food. The descriptions here sound like the powers of the dragon are used to wall in its people and encapsulate them for its propaganda machine. Conformity and allegiance are in the top tier of the dragon's "virtue" list.

WISDOM TO DISCERN IMPERSONATORS OF GOD

John describes beast #1 with language that sounds like Babylon and sounds like the dragon of 12:3, though beast #1 has "ten crowns" and the dragon only seven. Furthermore, the terms used (leopard, bear, lion) of beast #1 echo Daniel 7:1–7. Not to complicate this any more than we need to, but beast #1 sounds like the woman of Babylon who also had seven heads and ten horns and was full of blasphemy.

Satan is a deceiver, a liar. The agents of Satan deceive by impersonation. The animals impersonate Daniel, the wounded and healed beast impersonates the healing and resurrection of Jesus, the world follows the beast as people followed Jesus, the power and authority of the beast impersonates the Lamb's (4:11; 5:12–13; 7:12), the proud words echo Daniel 7:8's "little horn," beast #2 copies the Lamb's horns and the dragon's speech, does mighty signs that sound like the miracles of Jesus, and beast #2 has the power to give life to an image of the beast.

The singular mark of Babylon is arrogance to think it is the Eternal City, that it will never be defeated, and that it will never mourn (18:7). Rome, its goddess Roma, its embodiment in Babylon, the dragon, and the beasts act as if they are the god of this world. So arrogant they blaspheme God and God's name and the throne room and those in heaven (13:6). Arrogance and dominance evoke a hideous display of narcissism to the highest degree.

WISDOM TO DISCERN DECEPTIVE CONFORMITY

Rome was a vast, expanding empire. Rome's arrogance led it to believe its dominance was allegiance and popularity. What they were, however, was coerced conformity. The beasts of Revelation are described as having a massive following of the deceived. Not only does beast #1 have a throne, "the *whole world* was filled with wonder and followed the beast" and "worshiped the beast" (13:3–4). John says it was "given authority over every tribe, people, language and nation. All inhabitants of the earth will worship the beast" (13:7–8). The royal sycophant, beast #2, "made the earth and its inhabitants worship" beast #1 (13:12) and did miracles "in full view of the people" (13:13). The impact of beast #2's impersonations was that it "deceived the inhabitants of the earth" (13:14). Beast #2 used the powers of the empire to coerce "all people, great and small, rich and poor, free and slave, to receive a mark on their right hands or on their foreheads" (13:16).

Such supposed popularity is conformity, which deceives the world into thinking the beasts are for the people. All the while those with wisdom recognize deception, destruction, and death. The way of the dragon is death. Conformity in the Apocalypse leads to the dragon's den. "My way or the highway" emerges from the same sea as Beast #1.

Two Secrets

The descriptions of the beasts and dragon in today's passage mesmerize us at times to miss two little secret snippets that indicate that there's a victory coming for Team Lamb. First, beast #1 has the "authority to exercise its authority" but only for "forty-two months" (13:5). Again, three-and-a-half years. Just like 11:2–3; 12:6, 14, and each of these echo Daniel's "a time, times and half a time" (7:25). Some will drill down on a prediction of an exact 42 months, but this will not work for apocalyptic literature. These are the measures of a temporary period, in fact, a short period of time. A kind of "it won't last long."

The second secret has drawn extensive speculation. John explicitly states that beast #2's required "mark" is the "name of the beast," but its name is converted into a number. This is called "gematria" in Hebrew, and gematria converts the letters of a name into numbers. The number is 666, and this almost certainly refers to Nero. But first things: 7 is the complete, perfect number, and 6 is the imperfect, incomplete number. God is a 7 and humans are a 6. Here's a fact: Nerōn Kaisar (Greek) converted into numbers looks like this:

⇨ NRWN QSR = 50 + 200 + 6 + 50 + 100 + 60 + 200 = 666*

On top of this, many see a myth alive and well in the days of Domitian that Nero had not died but would return to be the emperor again, and this is perhaps at work in

---

* If the name is spelled "Nero Kaisar," it adds up to 616. And some manuscripts, instead of 666, have 616. Again, what are the odds?

Revelation 17:11. Not to make light of this, but what are the odds? Notice, too, that the mark impersonates the sealing of the Lamb's followers, who have his name on their forehead (14:1; 22:4).

The wisdom called for in verse eighteen is not the wisdom needed for a person to identify who this 666 might be. Instead, it is the wisdom to discern the power of the dragon at work in the beasts and, thus, to learn how to live as a witness and worshiper of the Lamb when surrounded by the dragon's Babylon and beasts.

QUESTIONS FOR REFLECTION AND APPLICATION

1. What shifts for you when you look at Revelation through a lens of discerning Babylon and beasts today, rather than asking who does what in this book?

2. What are some traits of antichrists?

3. What interpretations have you heard before about the Mark of the Beast?

THREE TRUTHS
TO EMBRACE

Revelation 14:1–20

THE 144,000

[1] *Then I looked, and there before me was the Lamb, standing on Mount Zion, and with him 144,000 who had his name and his Father's name written on their foreheads.* [2] *And I heard a sound from heaven like the roar of rushing waters and like a loud peal of thunder. The sound I heard was like that of harpists playing their harps.* [3] *And they sang a new song before the throne and before the four living creatures and the elders. No one could learn the song except the 144,000 who had been redeemed from the earth.* [4] *These are those who did not defile themselves with women, for they remained virgins. They follow the Lamb wherever he goes. They were purchased from among mankind and offered as firstfruits to God and the Lamb.* [5] *No lie was found in their mouths; they are blameless.*

THREE ANGELS WARN THE WORLD

[6] *Then I saw another **angel** flying in midair, and he had the eternal gospel to proclaim to those who live on the earth—to every*

nation, tribe, language and people. ⁷ He said in a loud voice, "Fear God and give him glory, because the hour of his judgment has come. Worship him who made the heavens, the earth, the sea and the springs of water."

⁸ A second **angel** followed and said, " 'Fallen! Fallen is Babylon the Great,' which made all the nations drink the maddening wine of her adulteries."

⁹ A third **angel** followed them and said in a loud voice: "If anyone worships the beast and its image and receives its mark on their forehead or on their hand, ¹⁰ they, too, will drink the wine of God's fury, which has been poured full strength into the cup of his wrath. They will be tormented with burning sulfur in the presence of the holy angels and of the Lamb. ¹¹ And the smoke of their torment will rise for ever and ever. There will be no rest day or night for those who worship the beast and its image, or for anyone who receives the mark of its name." ¹² This calls for patient endurance on the part of the people of God who keep his commands and remain faithful to Jesus.

¹³ Then I heard a voice from heaven say, "Write this: Blessed are the dead who die in the Lord from now on."

"Yes," says the Spirit, "they will rest from their labor, for their deeds will follow them."

JUDGMENT (WITH THREE MORE ANGELS)

¹⁴ I looked, and there before me was a white cloud, and seated on the cloud was one like a son of man with a crown of gold on his head and a sharp sickle in his hand. ¹⁵ Then another **angel** came out of the temple and called in a loud voice to him who was sitting on the cloud, "Take your sickle and reap, because the time to reap has come, for the harvest of the earth is ripe." ¹⁶ So

he who was seated on the cloud swung his sickle over the earth, and the earth was harvested.

[17] *Another **angel** came out of the temple in heaven, and he too had a sharp sickle.* [18] *Still another **angel**, who had charge of the fire, came from the altar and called in a loud voice to him who had the sharp sickle, "Take your sharp sickle and gather the clusters of grapes from the earth's vine, because its grapes are ripe."* [19] *The angel swung his sickle on the earth, gathered its grapes and threw them into the great winepress of God's wrath.* [20] *They were trampled in the winepress outside the city, and blood flowed out of the press, rising as high as the horses' bridles for a distance of 1,600 stadia.*

John loves to interrupt the flow of the three x seven disciplines or judgments. The seals were described in 6:1–8:1 and the trumpets in 8:2–11:19. Then we had an interruption to meet the woman's cosmic battle with the dragon. Then an interruption for the two beasts, and in chapter fourteen we get three more interruptions. Each interruption, and we did not mention those in chapters six through eleven, provides the believers in western Asia Minor with perspective on what is happening in God's world. Especially because it does not look like God's world at times!

In today's reading we encounter three separate interruptions that teach us three truths to embrace: (1) embrace those who are faithful to the Lamb; (2) embrace the call to follow the Lamb; and (3) embrace the reality of divine destruction of evil. Each of these sections of today's reading will have empowered the believers to walk faithfully with Babylon's hot breath on their trail. Each also taught the believers to live under the deeper reality that will follow in the seven bowls (15:1–16:21). Each is also a call to the listeners and readers to become accountable to the God who will bring justice to the world, ridding the world of its injustices, idolatries, and immoralities. Each also sweeps across the entirety of the story of Revelation—from the days of Jesus to New Jerusalem, reminding us that the Apocalypse does not glide on a chronological plane. One can read each of these episodes as mini-visions seen by John that he places here to keep the believers encouraged and stimulated to witness and worship.

EMBRACE THOSE WHO ARE FAITHFUL TO THE LAMB

Numbers, numbers, numbers. Revelation is full of them. Almost always symbolic though they are, these numbers have become invitations for speculations. Please return to chapter seven where this same group of 144,000 were described. There, I wrote that 144,000 is 1,000 x 12 x 12 and points us to a complete number of Israelites—and New Jerusalem, as we will see, is a cube of 12,000 stadia with walls of 144 cubits. I'm with the many who think 144,000, who are distinguished from an innumerable host of gentiles (7:9), represent the fullness of the *Jewish people of God who follow the Lamb.*

What stands out in today's passage about the 144,000 is (1) their *redemption song* to God. They are known for the name of the Lamb and Father; the sound of their harps accompanies their "new song" that no one but the 144,000 knows. We can leave it at that: we don't know the words of their song. Perhaps they are singing in Hebrew!

And (2) we learn of their whole life *witness*. It is not

uncommon to connect the abstinence from sex by the 144,000 to the ancient Israelite military requirement, which is why Brian Blount thinks the 144,000 are the "human wing of God's army" now fit for battle for the kingdom of God (Blount, *Revelation*, 145). Thus, perhaps they are like an ancient Israel military that does not have sex during wartime (cf. Deuteronomy 23:9–11; 2 Samuel 11:8–11). Perhaps they are involved in the third section of today's passage, the judgment of God (14:14–20). I'm not so sure. What stands out here is their abstinence from sex and their virginity (14:4). But, in the book of Revelation sex and idolatry, or immorality and idolatry, weave together into such a common idea from the ancient prophets that sexual activity fades. What matters is the worship of God that abandons the idolatries of Rome. Supporting this more symbolic meaning of abstinence is that they are worshiping God in song. John intensifies their witness to God in speaking of their being "purchased" as "firstfruits." Such expressions again take us to the importance of witness leading to martyrdom. Again, they tell the truth in their witness and John adds they are "blameless" in their Christian life.

The call here is for the listeners to embrace the truth that hundreds of thousands of Jewish believers have, are, and will continue to walk faithfully alongside the Lamb in their worship and witness. Some of their perfect number are already around the throne singing the songs of redemption.

EMBRACE THE CALL TO FOLLOW THE LAMB

The second section of today's passage describes three angels with three very brief sermons for believers. The first message is "the eternal gospel to proclaim" to the whole earth as witnesses (14:6). The proper response to this gospel is "Fear God and give him glory" and "worship" the Creator (14:7), revealing yet one more time the fundamental importance of worship for the Christian life. As well, this angel clarifies that the gospel message will extend to the ends of the earth and the numbers of those who turn to follow the Lamb will continue to expand. Those enduring injustice want to know that the dragon cannot thwart the work of God.

The second angel's message, an advance snapshot of Revelation 17:1–19:10, reveals the destiny of those who deal in idolatries, immoralities, and injustices. The words of the angel are "Fallen! Fallen is Babylon the Great" (14:8). Those who witness to and worship the Lamb need to know that Team Dragon will not rule the earth forever. God will. Something many of us need to remind ourselves of frequently.

Finally, the third angel warns the believers of the danger of capitulating to Babylon. Since Babylon's doom is sure, those who leave the way of the Lamb to follow the dragon will experience the final eradication that the dragon experiences (cf. 14:10–11 with 19:11–21 and 20:7–10). The language is fierce, gruesome, and over the top. We fail apocalyptic literature when we turn this language into a literal description of hell, Hades, or the eternal state of Team Dragon.

SPECIAL NOTE: John ends this second section in today's chapter in a way that explains why he glued these three angel messages together. The NIV's choice to keep verse twelve in a paragraph with vv. 9–11 confuses the reader. John turns here to challenge the believers in light of vv. 6–11. The proper response is "patient endurance," or resilience on the part of those who are devoted to the Lamb, that is, those who observe God's orders and are marked by Jesus-allegiance.

The promise is that the martyrs during these divine disciplines have the ultimate approval. They are "blessed" because they will, in the presence of the One on the throne and in the New Jerusalem, be refreshed from the labors of their discernments, their faithful witness, and their dissident worship. The deeds of their witness will follow them the way disciples follow their teacher (14:12–13).

EMBRACE THE JUDGMENT OF THE LAMB

Wise dissidents do not entangle themselves in vengeance as they ache for God to bring justice to the world. Revenge is easy. Grief-shaped hope for justice flows straight from the heart of our Creator. What I find challenging is precisely what Kirsten Powers wrote in a recent Substack newsletter. She had always prided herself in thinking she was not vengeful and was in fact a forgiving person, until she realized she . . . I'll let her say it:

> But the fact that I'm not actually enacting revenge does not make me not a vengeful person. I've just

outsourced it. Indeed if I'm totally honest, one of my most often cited Bible verses is, "Vengeance is the Lord's." I say it as a way to let go of any responsibility or need to hold a grudge. I thought that meant I wasn't vengeful until I came face to face with the fact that I do live with the expectation that consequences will come—of an expectation of vengeance.

I don't think desiring or seeking vengeance is wrong or right, especially when it's understood as a need to set things right. But we have to be honest that it does set a person up as the judge and jury. It requires a kind of separation that puts us above other people. It's fundamentally an ego-reinforcing desire, which as I've discussed is what I am trying to move away from. We need to remember also that whenever we ask for cosmic consequences for bad behavior, those consequences will be coming for us as much as they come for other people. So be careful what you wish for. (Powers, "What Fran Lebowitz . . .")

The bold and graphic images of judgment in Revelation, and surely 14:14–20 rises to near the top of the list, have purpose, and that purpose is neither punitive nor vengeful. Their purpose, as we have seen already, is disciplinary in that they evoke the opportunity to repent from the ways of Babylon. Their final aim is the eradication of all forms of evil in the world. When John chose to write an apocalypse with battles and victories and losses and tragedies, scenes like this one attended his decision. The connection of God and the Lamb to gruesome battle scenes can be disconcerting for many of us.

This third section of today's chapter again sketches

an alternative description of the downfall of Babylon. What I mean is that this is not a separate judgment from Revelation 17–19 but instead mirrors those chapters in advance. There are four actors: one "like a son of man," but this is *the* Son of Man from Daniel 7:13, and this Son of Man has not only a crown but the operative instrument for judgment: a sickle (Revelation 14:14), which occurs seven times in this passage. In 14:16 the cloud-riding Son of Man swings the sickle into the wheat field, as a glimpse of what is about to happen, and then an angel swings a sickle into the vineyard (14:19). Either there are two acts, one by the Son of Man and one by the third, yea sixth, angel of this passage; or, there is one act, one imaged by the Son of Man and one actually done by the angel. It is very possible the Son of Man's harvest reaps people for New Jerusalem while the angel's sickle is an act of judgment. The two acts describe the same, final judgment.

The angel's sickle administers the just anger of God against Team Dragon, depicted as a winepress shedding grape juices that flow so deep—hyperbole beyond hyperbole—the juices rise to the level of the bridle of horses—and the length of the river of blood, John calculates, as some one hundred and eighty miles. That's apocalyptic doing what only apocalyptic can do. As we continue to read Revelation together, we will see this kind of scene again in chapter sixteen's bowls, in the whole of 17:1–19:10, 19:17–21, 20:7–10, and the desires of the dragon, destruction and death, are tossed into the "lake of fire" (20:14). Gone. Evil will be eradicated for the New Jerusalem.

Not vengeance, but grief-shaped hope for justice.

FOR FURTHER READING

Kirsten Powers, "What Fran Lebowitz and the
    Enneagram Taught Me about My Need for
    Vengeance," https://kirstenpowers.substack.com
    /p/what-fran-lebowitz-and-the-enneagram.

THE GLORY SONG

Revelation 15:1–16:21

¹ *I saw in heaven another great and marvelous sign:* **seven angels with the seven last plagues**—*last, because with them God's wrath is completed.*

² *And I saw what looked like a sea of glass glowing with fire and, standing beside the sea, those who had been victorious over the beast and its image and over the number of its name. They held harps given them by God* ³ *and sang the song of God's servant Moses and of the Lamb:*

> "Great and marvelous are your deeds,
>   Lord God Almighty.
> Just and true are your ways,
>   King of the nations.
> 4 Who will not fear you, Lord,
>   and bring glory to your name?
> For you alone are holy.
> All nations will come
>   and worship before you,
> for your righteous acts have been revealed."

⁵ *After this I looked, and I saw in heaven the temple—that is, the tabernacle of the covenant law—and it was*

opened. ⁶ *Out of the temple came the seven angels with the seven plagues. They were dressed in clean, shining linen and wore golden sashes around their chests.* ⁷ *Then one of the four living creatures gave to the seven angels seven golden bowls filled with the wrath of God, who lives for ever and ever.* ⁸ *And the temple was filled with smoke from the glory of God and from his power, and no one could enter the temple until the seven plagues of the seven angels were completed.*

¹⁶:¹ *Then I heard a loud voice from the temple saying to the seven angels, "Go, pour out the seven bowls of God's wrath on the earth."*

² *The* **first angel** *went and poured out his bowl on the land, and ugly, festering sores broke out on the people who had the mark of the beast and worshiped its image.*

³ *The* **second angel** *poured out his bowl on the sea, and it turned into blood like that of a dead person, and every living thing in the sea died.*

⁴ *The* **third angel** *poured out his bowl on the rivers and springs of water, and they became blood.* ⁵ *Then I heard the angel in charge of the waters say:*

> *"You are just in these judgments, O Holy One,*
> *   you who are and who were;*
> ⁶ *for they have shed the blood of your holy people and*
> *   your prophets,*
> *and you have given them blood to drink as they*
> *   deserve."*

⁷ *And I heard the altar respond:*

> *"Yes, Lord God Almighty,*
> *true and just are your judgments."*

⁸ *The* **fourth angel** *poured out his bowl on the sun, and the*

sun was allowed to scorch people with fire. [9] They were seared by the intense heat and they cursed the name of God, who had control over these plagues, but they refused to repent and glorify him.

[10] The **fifth angel** poured out his bowl on the throne of the beast, and its kingdom was plunged into darkness. People gnawed their tongues in agony [11] and cursed the God of heaven because of their pains and their sores, but they refused to repent of what they had done.

[12] The **sixth angel** poured out his bowl on the great river Euphrates, and its water was dried up to prepare the way for the kings from the East. [13] Then I saw three impure spirits that looked like frogs; they came out of the mouth of the dragon, out of the mouth of the beast and out of the mouth of the false prophet. [14] They are demonic spirits that perform signs, and they go out to the kings of the whole world, to gather them for the battle on the great day of God Almighty.

[15] "Look, I come like a thief! Blessed is the one who stays awake and remains clothed, so as not to go naked and be shamefully exposed."

[16] Then they gathered the kings together to the place that in Hebrew is called Armageddon.

[17] The **seventh angel** poured out his bowl into the air, and out of the temple came a loud voice from the throne, saying, "It is done!" [18] Then there came flashes of lightning, rumblings, peals of thunder and a severe earthquake. No earthquake like it has ever occurred since mankind has been on earth, so tremendous was the quake. [19] The great city split into three parts, and the cities of the nations collapsed. God remembered Babylon the Great and gave her the cup filled with the wine of the fury of his wrath. [20] Every island fled away and the mountains could not be found. [21] From the sky huge hailstones, each weighing about a hundred pounds, fell on people. And they cursed God on account of the plague of hail, because the plague was so terrible.

All these interludes and interruptions can cause us to lose our way as we read the book of Revelation. But John interrupts the unfolding of divine disciplines, not to derail us but to guide us in our listening or reading. Once again, the interlude at 15:2–8 (in bold in the Scripture passage) reshapes how we hear the pouring out of the seven bowls of divine wrath against evil. Before John is willing to describe for us what he saw about the seven bowls, he lays before us a scene of those who "had been victorious over the beast and its image and over the number [=666] of its name" and the song they sang to God in praise.

THE GLORY SONG

One word, appearing twice and in both halves of this interlude, sums up what John wants his listeners to hear. The word is "glory" (15:4, 8). The seven bowls will bring glory to God, not because of revenge but because the world will be put to rights, will be back in designed order of creation. There's more. The seven bowls anticipate the defeat of Babylon (17:1–19:21). The fifth, sixth, and seventh bowls are judgments on the beast, Babylon's river (the Euphrates), and Babylon itself (16:10–21). Two reasons shape these judgments. First, to eliminate evil and opposition to God and the Lamb. Second, to make the world fit for New Jerusalem. The first without the second is vengeance. The second without the first is wishful utopianism. The first with the second establishes justice.

The establishment of justice in God's world for God's people brings God final glory (15:4, 8). The word "glory" appears seventeen times in Revelation. The main purpose of the term is to point both (1) to who God is and (2) to what God deserves for what God has done through the

Lamb in eliminating evil and establishing justice. The four living creatures give God glory and sing to God (4:9, 11) just as a multitude of angels and creatures great and small give glory to the Lamb for his victorious redemption (5:12, 13; 7:12). Even the opponents of the Lamb are called to give God glory (15:8) and the conquered turn to give God the glory (11:13). The Lamb's victory over Babylon leads to a unified praise of glory (19:1, 7). Perhaps the most stimulating verse of all is found in 21:11 where we learn that New Jerusalem glows "with the glory of God, and its brilliance" is like precious jewels. New Jerusalem needs neither sun nor moon because God illuminates the city (21:23). Even the "glory and honor of the nations will be brought" into New Jerusalem to enhance the glory of God (21:26).

So, the song of those who conquer the dragon's push toward death and destruction, those who gain victories over sin and systemic injustices, rehearses that it was not their victory but God's. God's ways are "just and true," and all will honor and revere God and "bring glory to your name" (15:3–4). So expansive is the impact of those who conquer Babylon's ways that "all nations will come and worship" God and the Lamb (15:4). The word glory sums up that song.

In heaven John sees a "temple" (15:5, 6, 8). The word translated "temple" in the NIV is better translated "sanctuary" or (as Ian Paul translates it, "tent of meeting"; Paul, *Revelation*, 263). But it is combined very cleverly with the word "witness" so in *The Second Testament* I translate it as "the witness-tent's sanctuary." Don't skip over this: this expression describes the place where the Lamb's witnesses gather in heaven to sing forever the glories of God's just making of the world. One has to wonder if this sanctuary is not the heavenly template of New Jerusalem. Their witness, buttressed with their prayers for "How long?" (6:9–11), suddenly provides us deeper perspective of what is about to occur in the seven bowls: the heaven-dressed prayers of the oppressed emerge from their sanctuary to undo the injustices on earth. So effusive and effulgent was the glory of God as the mission to bring justice was issued to the seven angels that God's glory filled up heaven with "smoke" (15:8).

I emphasize the glory of God in order to ward off the instinct so many have to gloat over the judgments of God and to speculate about who they think most deserves these judgments. Both of these approaches for reading the seven bowls fail to grapple with the intensity of the prayers for justice, the unraveling of injustice, and the magnificence of a final justice. Instead of calculating the science of what happens when the land, the sea, the water supplies, and the sun fail to provide for humans, we need to see God at work here to eradicate evil as embodied in the dragon, the beast, and Babylon. *So New Jerusalem can dwell in peace!*

EARTH

The first four and seventh of the seven bowls, also described as plagues (cf. 9:18, 20; 11:6; 13:3, 12, 14; 15:1, 6, 8; 16:9, 21; 18:4, 8; 21:9; 22:18), turn the earth against itself: the "land" (16:2 is the same as NIV's "earth" in 16:1), the sea, water supplies, and the sun. Add to this that the seventh bowl judges the "air" in such a manner that an earthquake erupts in the "great city," that is "Babylon" (16:19). So powerful was the earthquake that John sees islands dispersing and mountains collapsing (16:20). Connected to the air judgment and the earthquake, John sees "huge hailstones, each weighing about one hundred pounds" falling out of the sky onto humans (16:21).

Babylon Today: War Machines

The blessing of Jesus on peacemakers ought at least challenge the war machine nations of the west, led as they are by the war technology and developments in the USA. When we compare ourselves to the ancient Roman empire's ruthless war machine, we must conclude that we are more like them than not like them.

From the Peter G. Peterson Foundation:

Defense spending by the United States accounted for nearly 40 percent of military expenditures by countries around the world in 2022, according to recently released figures from the Stockholm International Peace Research Institute (SIPRI). U.S. defense spending increased by $71 billion from 2021 to 2022, in part due to a military aid sent to support Ukraine in its ongoing conflict, and the United States now spends more on defense than the next 10 countries combined (up from outspending the next 9 countries combined in 2021).

SIPRI's definition of defense spending is broader than the definitions that are most frequently used in fiscal policy discussions in the United States, and according to their calculations, the United States spent $877 billion on national defense in 2022. SIPRI includes discretionary and mandatory outlays by the Department of Defense, Department of Energy, Department of State, and the National Intelligence Program. By contrast, the national defense budget function ($766 billion in 2022) excludes outlays by the Department of State and certain programs of the Department of Energy. Nonetheless, the SIPRI comparison provides useful insights on the sheer scale of U.S. defense spending relative to other nations.

Although the United States spends more on defense than any other country, the Congressional Budget Office projects that defense spending as a share of gross domestic product (GDP) will decline over the next 10 years—from 3.1 percent of GDP in 2023 to 2.8 percent in 2033. That is considerably lower than the 50-year average spending on defense of 4.3 percent of GDP.

https://www.pgpf.org/blog/2023/04/the-united-states-spends-more-on-defense-than-the-next-10-countries-combined.

For the Department of Defense's numbers: https://www.usaspending.gov/agency/department-of-defense?fy=2023.

For Wikipedia: https://en.wikipedia.org/wiki/Military_budget_of_the_United_States.

BABYLON

The seven bowls concentrate, unlike the seals and the trumpets, on Babylon, a name and city that represents tyranny, arrogance, violence, economic exploitation, and war. The fifth bowl is poured out on the unrepentant and unrepenting "throne of the beast," namely, the emperors of Rome (16:10–11).

The sixth is poured out on Babylon's famous river, its water supply (16:12–16). This sixth bowl is like an origami art piece unfolding into the previously unknown and unheard of. Euphrates withers into dry land so the "kings from the East" can march on Jerusalem. A grotesque little Golum-like image occurs next: three frogs, or impure spirits, come from the mouth of the dragon and the "false prophet." A false prophet has not appeared until now but will appear again in 19:20 and 20:10, and this false prophet's "signs" lead us to identify it as beast #2 (13:11–18). Its triple "demonic spirits" lead the "kings of the whole world" to arm themselves for "the battle on the great day of God Almighty," which refers to the time of the Second Coming. John says they will gather at "Armageddon," which means "Mount Megiddo." The Jezreel Valley below Megiddo featured many ancient battles. The term does not point to a literal place with a literal battle. It's a trope for a decisive battlefield (2 Kings 9:27; 2 Chronicles 35:22; Zechariah 12:11).

Many combine this battle with Revelation 14:17–20 (blood up to the horses' bridles) and 19:11–20. Most of what is said today about the Battle of Armageddon comes from one speculation piled on top of another on top of others. This much-used title then has become an apocalyptic myth found in all sorts of sermons and books.* A wiser reading advocates seeing all the final battle scenes as tropes for erasing evil and oppression in order to establish a lasting justice and peace in God's world.

The fifth, sixth, and seventh bowl, poured out on the dragon, its beasts, and Babylon, leads directly into John's vision of the fall of Babylon, which we began to discuss on page 183. With our reflections on Revelation's seventeenth chapter already done, I will now turn to the eighteenth and some of the nineteenth chapter.

For our reflections on the marks of Babylon in Revelation 17, see page 26.

QUESTIONS FOR REFLECTION AND APPLICATION

1. What brings glory to God in the Apocalypse?

2. What do you notice about God's justice and judgment in this section?

---

* For a standard example, see the description of J.D. Pentecost here: https://en.wikipedia.org/wiki/Armageddon (accessed, 15 May 2023).

3. Look up the words of "sanctuary" in Revelation and ask one question: Is the reference pointing to New Jerusalem? See Revelation 3:12; 7:15; 11:1–2, 19; 14:15, 17; 15:5–8; 16:1, 17; 21:22.

4. What are the consequences for God's enemies in the end?

5. How does it impact your reading of Revelation to see the battle imagery as symbolism of God's work for justice?

BEFORE NEW
JERUSALEM CAN ARRIVE

Revelation 18:1–19:10

*¹ After this I saw another angel coming down from heaven. He
had great authority, and the earth was illuminated by his splendor. ² With a mighty voice he shouted:*

> " 'Fallen! Fallen is Babylon the Great!'
>> She has become a dwelling for demons
> and a haunt for every impure spirit,
>> a haunt for every unclean bird,
>> a haunt for every unclean and detestable animal.
> ³ For all the nations have drunk
>> the maddening wine of her adulteries.
> The kings of the earth committed adultery with her,
> and the merchants of the earth grew rich from her
>> excessive luxuries."

⁴ Then I heard another voice from heaven say:

> " 'Come out of her, my people,'
>> so that you will not share in her sins,
>> so that you will not receive any of her plagues;

⁵ *for her sins are piled up to heaven,*
  and God has remembered her crimes.
⁶ *Give back to her as she has given;*
  pay her back double for what she has done.
  Pour her a double portion from her own cup.
⁷ *Give her as much torment and grief*
  as the glory and luxury she gave herself.
In her heart she boasts,
  'I sit enthroned as queen.
I am not a widow;
  I will never mourn.'
⁸ *Therefore in one day her plagues will overtake her:*
  death, mourning and famine.
She will be consumed by fire,
  for mighty is the Lord God who judges her.

⁹ "When the kings of the earth who committed adultery with her and shared her luxury see the smoke of her burning, they will weep and mourn over her. ¹⁰ Terrified at her torment, they will stand far off and cry:

  " 'Woe! Woe to you, great city,
    you mighty city of Babylon!
  In one hour your doom has come!'

¹¹ "The merchants of the earth will weep and mourn over her because no one buys their cargoes anymore—¹² cargoes of gold, silver, precious stones and pearls; fine linen, purple, silk and scarlet cloth; every sort of citron wood, and articles of every kind made of ivory, costly wood, bronze, iron and marble; ¹³ cargoes of cinnamon and spice, of incense, myrrh and frankincense, of wine and olive oil, of fine flour and wheat; cattle and sheep; horses and carriages; and human beings sold as slaves.

[14] *"They will say, 'The fruit you longed for is gone from you. All your luxury and splendor have vanished, never to be recovered.'* [15] *The merchants who sold these things and gained their wealth from her will stand far off, terrified at her torment. They will weep and mourn* [16] *and cry out:*

> *" 'Woe! Woe to you, great city,*
> > *dressed in fine linen, purple and scarlet,*
> > *and glittering with gold, precious stones and pearls!*
> [17] *In one hour such great wealth has been brought to ruin!'*

"Every sea captain, and all who travel by ship, the sailors, and all who earn their living from the sea, will stand far off. [18] *When they see the smoke of her burning, they will exclaim, 'Was there ever a city like this great city?'* [19] *They will throw dust on their heads, and with weeping and mourning cry out:*

> *" 'Woe! Woe to you, great city,*
> > *where all who had ships on the sea*
> > *became rich through her wealth!*
> *In one hour she has been brought to ruin!'*
> [20] *"Rejoice over her, you heavens!*
> > *Rejoice, you people of God!*
> > *Rejoice, apostles and prophets!*
> *For God has judged her*
> *with the judgment she imposed on you."*

[21] *Then a mighty angel picked up a boulder the size of a large millstone and threw it into the sea, and said:*

> *"With such violence*
> > *the great city of Babylon will be thrown down,*
> > *never to be found again.*

²² *The music of harpists and musicians, pipers and*
      trumpeters,
   will never be heard in you again.
No worker of any trade
   will ever be found in you again.
The sound of a millstone
   will never be heard in you again.
²³ *The light of a lamp*
   will never shine in you again.
The voice of bridegroom and bride
   will never be heard in you again.
Your merchants were the world's important people.
   By your magic spell all the nations were led astray.
²⁴ *In her was found the blood of prophets and of God's*
      holy people,
of all who have been slaughtered on the earth."

^{19:1} *After this I heard what sounded like the roar of a great*
multitude in heaven shouting:

"Hallelujah!
Salvation and glory and power belong to our God,
   ² *for true and just are his judgments.*
He has condemned the great prostitute
   who corrupted the earth by her adulteries.
He has avenged on her the blood of his servants."

³ *And again they shouted:*

"Hallelujah!
The smoke from her goes up for ever and ever."

⁴ *The twenty-four elders and the four living creatures fell*

down and worshiped God, who was seated on the throne. And they cried:

"Amen, Hallelujah!"

⁵ *Then a voice came from the throne, saying:*

"Praise our God,
all you his servants,
you who fear him,
both great and small!"

⁶ *Then I heard what sounded like a great multitude, like the roar of rushing waters and like loud peals of thunder, shouting:*

"Hallelujah!
For our Lord God Almighty reigns.
⁷ *Let us rejoice and be glad*
and give him glory!
For the wedding of the Lamb has come,
and his bride has made herself ready.
⁸ *Fine linen, bright and clean,*
was given her to wear."

(Fine linen stands for the righteous acts of God's holy people.)
⁹ *Then the angel said to me, "Write this: Blessed are those who are invited to the wedding supper of the Lamb!" And he added, "These are the true words of God."*

¹⁰ *At this I fell at his feet to worship him. But he said to me, "Don't do that! I am a fellow servant with you and with your brothers and sisters who hold to the testimony of Jesus. Worship God! For it is the Spirit of prophecy who bears testimony to Jesus."*

One of the most Christian acts we can perform today centers on rejoicing over the collapse of injustices. Whether it is the (beginning of the) defeat of slavery in *The Emancipation Proclamation*, the defeat of Hitler in World War II, the knocking down of the Berlin wall, or the end of Apartheid in South Africa. We should throw a party, pop the cork of champagne, serve the food, crank up the music, do some high-stepping on the dance floor, and give everyone around high fives and hugs. Celebrating the end of any injustice turns our hearts away from suffering and oppression while it sets our hope on a new day when justice and peace will roar like a river over a massive waterfall. Lesser victories, at least from the angle of global changes, like the unraveling of a corrupted leader's sins of power and sexual abuse, the passing of an employment law to outlaw systemic violence against people of color, a life-saving divorce from an abusive spouse, or a judge's guilty verdict in a murder—all these deserve celebration.

Yet, any celebration of victory over violence carries the stings of memory, oppressions, tortures, violence, and death. Hitler's defeat does not deny the chilling experience of demonic evil in the Holocaust's concentration camps, nor does it raise from the dead the millions murdered. Nor will the sacking of a pastor erase the haunting memories of sexual abuse or stop triggering the trauma. Nor does an employment law alter the economic imbalance formed over generations among America's people of color. Celebration and trauma tie themselves together into a tight knot.

These two—celebration and trauma—are intertwined in the whole of today's passage. The joy of song and dance with "Fallen! Fallen is Babylon the Great!" (18:2) does not erase the memory of persecution and prayers for justice by the martyrs in 6:9–11. Speaking of memory, so powerful is the desire for Babylon's collapse that John writes up his vision with more than a few echoes of the fall of Tyre in Ezekiel 27 and the collapse of Babylon in Jeremiah 25. John tells the story of two women (Revelation 12 and 17–19) and two cities (17–19 and 20–22).

I have emphasized reading Revelation as a narrative that will not tolerate reading the seals, trumpets, and bowls as acts of revenge. Instead, they are divine disciplines that call humans to the way of the Lamb, that will not accept the violence of evil, that will not stop until justice arrives, and will lead us all in a song of praise to the all-glorious God and the Lamb in New Jerusalem. But that narrative in Revelation entailed pain, suffering, and martyrdom. The Apocalypse of John fashions no utopian pie-eyed song of endless progress and upward and onward with our chins up and our chests puffed out. No, it stories for us a sometimes brutal reality that eventually turns an eternal corner into a peace-soaked Eternal City, the New Jerusalem (not Rome).

In what follows I will concentrate on the poetic lines of today's reading, and the lines will be sorted by themes. Call these the themes of the oppressed, and they can be sorted into two themes: Doom and Joy.

Songs of Doom

No passage in all of Revelation reveals the nature of dissident discipleship more than today's passage. Here we have a small group of marginalized believers in Jesus in western Asia Minor, huddled in house groups, reading and listening to the Bible and apostolic teachings, uniting in fellowship, stumbling along in theology and leadership, and singing songs about the Lamb and that God is the world's true God. In our passage we encounter poetic lines that turn from wondering what to do to courageous, bold, and extravagant prophetic denunciations of Rome (Babylon). Such was the life of a dissident disciple of the Lamb.

The martyrs of the early church, who have voices at times in Revelation (e.g., 6:9–11; 7:1–16; 8:3; 11:1–14; 12:17; 13:7, 15–27; 14:1–6; 15:2; 17:6), ache for God to intervene, stop the oppressions and violence against them, and long for the day when God's New Jerusalem will be the way of the world. They know pain when they sing the songs of doom in today's passage because they celebrate out of their trauma. A trauma that they will never forget but a trauma from which they will heal. So John goes total apocalyptic and pronounces the fall of Rome, or Babylon, and *does so with such gusto that he puts it all in the past tense.* Not "will fall" but has "fallen" (18:2).

The language of doom runs through six separate sections in Revelation 18. First, they rejoice that Babylon is "fallen" and will be left desolate, a theme very common in the prophets (18:2, 5, 8, 9, 17, 19, 20, 21–24; Isaiah 13:21; Jeremiah 9:10). Babylon thought it was invincible and so did Tyre. But even more, Rome saw itself as the eternal city and its power, domination, military, arrogance, and economic exploitation created one of the world's longest lasting empires. But empires rise, empires fall—what happened to Babylon and Tyre happened to Rome. Every Babylon will rise to its zenith and then fall. So, too, will our country. Only one City is truly Eternal, New Jerusalem. The timeliness and timelessness of John's exposé of Babylon led a recent author to observe that "although John reports his vision in terms that make clear connections with first-century life, the result is a curiously contemporary critique of power and wealth in human empires of every age" (Paul, *Revelation*, 301).

Second, their doom song assails those who were complicit in Babylon's sins (Revelation 18:3). John sets the scene for the doom song in 18:16–17 with a lengthy list of the details of Rome's/Babylon's economic exploitation from such faraway places as Spain and China and Africa and India (18:11–15). Ian Paul says this list of cargo "feels a little like a tour round a grand house of one of the wealthy elite in Rome itself" (Paul, *Revelation*, 289). But the complicity of the merchants and sea captains goes unacknowledged, so they turn, wailing and woe-ing (18:10, 16, 19) over Babylon's *and their* losses. The last "cargo" mentioned reveals the depth of Rome's exploitation: "and human beings sold as slaves" (18:13). Babylon's trafficking has no boundaries. Gordon Fee's remark remains relevant: "this list is not about the shoemaker or the baker or the household slave. This is about the fabulously wealthy, those who in every culture consider themselves as worth all they get, and who very often consider the rest of the world as somewhere beneath them" (Fee, *Revelation*, 255). Rome's victories, called extending the *pax Romana*, were military dominance, intimidation, and exploitation. Rome's economy needed slaves. The places conquered became fertile for shipping future slaves. New World slavery imitated Rome centuries later. Their grief, then, is as much over their own losses as Babylon's.

Third, their songs of doom recall the depth and width and height of Babylon's sins (18:5, 9–20). Fourth, doom means Babylon's corruptions will reverse direction, returning only to fall upon Babylon (18:6–8, 16–17, 20, 21–24). Fifth, the song of doom continues with the act of a "mighty angel" (18:21–24). Babylon's end is permanent, a kind of hyperbole characteristic of prophetic warnings. Babylon is "never to be found again" and there's no longer music in the city, and no more commerce, and no more nightly glittering lights, and no more wedding celebrations. The descriptions remind me of images I have seen online of former Olympic stadiums now filled with wild animals and weeds and broken windows. Finally, the martyrs and murders of Babylon appear yet again (18:24). Babylon falls because "in her was found the blood of prophets and of God's holy people, of all who have been slaughtered on the earth."

Revelation 18, in its songs of doom, rehearses the marks of Babylon's corruptions in Revelation 17. The doom songs are the heart cries of the oppressed now relieved by their answers, as I explained to open today's passage.

SONGS OF JOY

As there were six doom songs, so there are six poetic lines of joy—not so long. One can see these as antiphonal responses to the doom songs. The lines of joy appear in 19:1–2, 3, 4, 5, 6–8, and finish off with a blessing buckled down with "These are the true words of God" (19:9). In other words, the doom of the dragon is sure.

The joy songs begin with a rich celebration of words. Not only is there the common "Hallelujah!" but also "Salvation and glory and power belong to our God [not to the dragon nor to its beasts and city]" (19:1). God's judgments, the "great multitude in heaven" roars, are "true and just" because he has brought down the perpetrators of violence, injustice, destruction, and death. Followed by cascading hallelujahs in 19:3, 4, and 6, along with a "Praise our God" on the part of some voice "from the throne" (but not God's voice; 19:5). If the opening joy song was rich in theology, the last major joy song takes us into the final visions about the New Jerusalem. Not only does the last song have another "Hallelujah" but it announces that "our Lord God Almighty reigns." Here's the new part: "for the wedding of the Lamb has come and his bride has made herself ready. Fine linen, bright and clean, was given her to wear" (19:7–8).

Attached to the wedding announcement comes an invitation: "Blessed are those who are invited to the wedding supper of the Lamb!" (19:9).

John is so overcome, he falls down to worship the angel who revealed all these visions to him. The angel tells John to stop because he (the angel) is but a witness to the Lamb as well. He was but a servant on a ladder from the throne room to planet earth to John and the churches (19:10; cf. 1:1–3).

The joy songs are not *Schadenfreude*, that is, rejoicing in the enemy's downfall, gloating like the Roman military when it conquered a new city. Instead, these joy songs are trauma-born expressions of a justice now made real, and a justice that reverses the script of those who perpetrated the injustices, destructions, exploitations, and deaths.

QUESTIONS FOR REFLECTION
AND APPLICATION

1. How do celebration and trauma stand in tension when justice finally happens?

2. What do the songs of doom communicate?

3. What do the songs of joy communicate?

4. If you were to write an honest song of doom, judgement, and downfall of enemies, what would you sing?

5. What are some victories God has accomplished in your life that you want to celebrate with joy?

FAITHFUL AND TRUE

Revelation 19:11–21

[11] *I saw heaven standing open and there before me was a white horse, whose rider is called Faithful and True. With justice he judges and wages war.* [12] *His eyes are like blazing fire, and on his head are many crowns. He has a name written on him that no one knows but he himself.* [13] *He is dressed in a robe dipped in blood, and his name is the Word of God.* [14] *The armies of heaven were following him, riding on white horses and dressed in fine linen, white and clean.* [15] *Coming out of his mouth is a sharp sword with which to strike down the nations. "He will rule them with an iron scepter." He treads the winepress of the fury of the wrath of God Almighty.* [16] *On his robe and on his thigh he has this name written:*

KING OF KINGS AND LORD OF LORDS.

[17] *And I saw an angel standing in the sun, who cried in a loud voice to all the birds flying in midair, "Come, gather together for the great supper of God,* [18] *so that you may eat the flesh of kings, generals, and the mighty, of horses and their riders, and the flesh of all people, free and slave, great and small."*
[19] *Then I saw the beast and the kings of the earth and their armies gathered together to wage war against the rider on the*

horse and his army. ²⁰ But the beast was captured, and with it the false prophet who had performed the signs on its behalf. With these signs he had deluded those who had received the mark of the beast and worshiped its image. The two of them were thrown alive into the fiery lake of burning sulfur. ²¹ The rest were killed with the sword coming out of the mouth of the rider on the horse, and all the birds gorged themselves on their flesh.

In reading Revelation, one cannot be surprised by sudden interruptions or with reports of a simpler, shorter vision that recaptures and even remixes previous or future visions in the book. Today's passage is one such remix. First, it sends me on a long trip back to Revelation 1's vision of Jesus and then straight on to 3:14 where Jesus is the "faithful and true witness." Then it takes me to Revelation 5's Lion morphing into a Lamb, and then also to Revelation 14:14–20's Son of Man, not to mention the many times songs are sung to Jesus the Lord. Each of the scenes is distinct, shifting to new titles and themes and actions. Today's passage adds more than its share.

But this passage also shifts in its description of the fall of Babylon. The mighty empire of Rome, unlike all its other battles, meets more than its match in the Word-Sword of the Lamb of God. So this passage remixes Revelation 17:1–19:10.

WHO IS JESUS?

Read today's passage with me as I scout out descriptions of Jesus. They tumble off the page onto our notebooks and screens: on a white horse, called "Faithful and True," and he will judge "with justice." His eyes are like blazing fire, and he has many crowns on his head—don't you wonder how one balances many crowns while riding a horse down-hill from heaven? His robe is "dipped in blood," which evokes his crucifixion and resurrection. In his trail are the "armies of heaven" who are also riding white (pure, holy) horses and dressed up in a "white and clean" outfit.

His names are varied in the passage: "no one knows but he himself" his name, yet his name is "Word of God"—does this leak the name? And he is called "King of Kings and Lord of Lords" (19:11–16).

Here is a challenge for each of us: Is our Jesus that wild but necessary combination of love and justice, of peace and defeat? Is our Jesus one whose death and resurrection morphs him from a Lion into a Lamb who defeats destruction and death with the Word of God? Or, have we fallen for a Marvel movie form of violence that breaks down the goodness of God in the face of the Son of God? Today's passage challenges us to hold two tense poles in one hand. It's a challenge at times, not least when we are the ones wanting vengeance.

WHAT WILL JESUS DO?

His weapon is, to be sure, a "sharp sword." But notice the powerful shift: his sword is not in his fist, nor does he wield it as the armies of Rome. Rather, the sword of this king emerges from his mouth because it is the Word of God! He will strike down Team Dragon who refuse repentance (cf. 16:11) as Jesus "treads the winepress of the fury of the wrath of God Almighty" (19:15). Wrath in the Bible is God's turning humans over to the consequences of their own sins (Romans 1:18–32), and it is not God pitching a fit at someone for offending him. Sorry for the language, but it works here.

No, Jesus returns to rule over all creation and nations and tongues and tribes. And he will conquer with a Mouth-Sword, which is John's figurative language for the Word of God's power to slay the heart of the unrepentant. The victory over Team Dragon, over Babylon, shifts from "fallen" to a supper of devouring the enemies by nothing less than "all the birds flying in midair" (19:17–18). Gruesome, to be sure. Battle scenes were common in the ancient world, common enough that authors could capture the gory details into prophecies, and this one comes straight out of Ezekiel:

> "Son of man, this is what the Sovereign LORD says: Call out to every kind of bird and all the wild animals:
> 'Assemble and come together from all around to the sacrifice I am preparing for you, the great sacrifice on the mountains of Israel. There you will eat flesh and drink blood. You will eat the flesh of mighty men and drink the blood of the princes of the earth as if they were rams and lambs, goats and bulls—all of them fattened animals from Bashan. At the sacrifice I am preparing for you, you will eat fat till you are glutted and drink blood till you are drunk. At my table you will eat your fill of horses and riders, mighty men and soldiers of every kind,' declares the Sovereign LORD. (Ezekiel 39:17–20)

Birds of prey have always found corpses, carcasses, garbage, and roadkill.

The gory scene of birds of prey feasting on Team Dragon, which had the equivalent impact as covering one's eyes in a movie theater for many, turns into an explanation of how the enemies of God were defeated. Team Dragon-inspired armies, led by beast #1, gather to battle with the White Horse Rider but both beast #1 and #2 are captured by Team Lamb (Word of God), and—more gruesome—"thrown alive into the fiery lake of burning sulfur" (19:20). This, as well as the Mouth-Sword (Word of God) inflicted death of all of the beasts' armies, signifies the eradication of evil and the workers of injustice, violence, exploitation, and enslavement. They will be joined by the dragon in 20:10.

Who is Jesus? The Word of God who slays with the Word. What does he do? Vanquishes evil *for one reason and one reason alone: to establish the kingdom of God, the New Jerusalem, a kingdom of justice and peace.* To establish a just world, an unjust system must be disestablished. The disruption does not come by manipulation and machination but by the Word from the mouth of the one who is faithful and true.

QUESTIONS FOR REFLECTION AND APPLICATION

1. How does this passage repeat themes from earlier in the book?

2. What is the significance of Jesus' sword coming out of his mouth?

DESTROYING THE DRAGON AND DEATH

Revelation 20:1–15

DRAGON'S DESTRUCTION

¹ *And* **I saw** *an angel coming down out of heaven, having the key to the Abyss and holding in his hand a great chain.* ² *He seized the dragon, that ancient serpent, who is the devil, or Satan, and bound him for a thousand years.* ³ *He threw him into the Abyss, and locked and sealed it over him, to keep him from deceiving the nations anymore until the thousand years were ended. After that, he must be set free for a short time.*

⁴ **I saw** *thrones on which were seated those who had been given authority to judge. And I saw the souls of those who had been beheaded because of their testimony about Jesus and because of the word of God. They had not worshiped the beast or its image and had not received its mark on their foreheads or their hands. They came to life and reigned with Christ a thousand years.* ⁵ *(The rest of the dead did not come to life until the thousand years were ended.) This is the first resurrection.* ⁶ *Blessed and holy are those who share in the first resurrection. The second death has no power over them, but they will be priests of God and of Christ and will reign with him for a thousand years.*

⁷ *When the thousand years are over, Satan will be released from his prison* ⁸ *and will go out to deceive the nations in the four corners of the earth—Gog and Magog—and to gather them for battle. In number they are like the sand on the seashore.* ⁹ *They marched across the breadth of the earth and surrounded the camp of God's people, the city he loves. But fire came down from heaven and devoured them.* ¹⁰ *And the devil, who deceived them, was thrown into the lake of burning sulfur, where the beast and the false prophet had been thrown. They will be tormented day and night for ever and ever.*

DEATH'S DESTRUCTION

¹¹ *Then I saw a great white throne and him who was seated on it. The earth and the heavens fled from his presence, and there was no place for them.* ¹² *And I saw the dead, great and small, standing before the throne, and books were opened. Another book was opened, which is the book of life. The dead were judged according to what they had done as recorded in the books.* ¹³ *The sea gave up the dead that were in it, and death and Hades gave up the dead that were in them, and each person was judged according to what they had done.* ¹⁴ *Then death and Hades were thrown into the lake of fire. The lake of fire is the second death.* ¹⁵ *Anyone whose name was not found written in the book of life was thrown into the lake of fire.*

Revelation is the story of everything, the entire cosmos from creation to New Jerusalem. For a new creation to occur, the old creation must be redeemed and transformed or eliminated. The way of the dragon is the way of death. For final life to arrive, the dragon's pill of death must be eradicated. From the sixth chapter through the twentieth chapter one form of the dragon's rebellion after another meets its match in the victory of the Lamb, a victory to establish justice and eternal life. We are near the end of the battles of Team Dragon against Team Lamb. With the two beasts and their armies defeated, two final tasks remain: capturing and destroying both the dragon and death. Death, in fact, is the ultimate human enemy and the dragon is death's agent. Today's reading turns the Lamb's forces against the final two enemies of the cosmos.

DEFEATING THE DRAGON

The dragon is defeated in two stages. In the first stage, an angel descends from the throne room with the mission of grabbing the dragon by the neck, shoving it into prison and, under lock and key, the cosmos breathes, for a temporary period, life on earth without the dragon and death (20:1–6). It is a tragedy that so many read this passage to debate issues about the "millennium" and so miss what this passage is about: the first stage of the dragon's destruction. Brian Blount's quip about the millennium deserves to be read more than once: "too much has been made of a concept [millennium] to which John gave very little attention" (Blount, *Revelation*, 366). This is the *only* passage about a 1,000-year reign on the earth in the whole Bible. So we need to be cautious.

STAGE ONE

Here is a delicious irony. *Those who reign on earth in the millennium are martyrs*, that is, those whom the dragon, the beasts, and Babylon have put to death. The millennial is the great script-flip of Revelation. The dragon goes to prison and the imprisoned who were put to death gain the freedom to rule the world instead of the dragon. In the history of Christian thinking, some have claimed the martyrs (20:4) represent all Christians, but: (1) that's not true, as martyrs don't represent everyone in the Apocalypse; and (2) using them to represent everyone degrades the witness of those who have actually given their lives as dissidents of Babylon. Using them as representatives is nothing less than witness appropriation, like cultural, ethnic, or racial appropriations in our society today.

Reading this passage leads me to give God thanks for those who have gone before us, who are now with us, and those who will be after us. Those I have in mind are the ones who have witnessed courageously for Jesus and about Jesus in the heat of Team Dragon and who have paid the price of life. They died "because of their testimony [=witness] about Jesus and because of the word of God" (20:4; cf. 1:2, 9; 6:9; 12:11, 17; 19:10).

Christian thinking about the millennium has often been understood as a literal 1,000-year rule of Christ on earth. Even more, many Christians add all the physical, earthly, and Jerusalem-based prophecies of the Old Testament to mushroom them into an absolutely wonderful utopia on planet earth. But, John's big on symbolism through numbers. One thousand represents a long time, but it is not eternity. So, what we have in this millennium passage concerns a temporary state of affairs: the dragon is in prison and those murdered by Team Dragon are ruling. When did or when is or when will this happen?

Consider this: In Revelation 12 we saw the defeat of the dragon who was then cast down to earth. Maybe the angel's seizing of the dragon to open up today's passage remixes the dragon's being sent to earth in Revelation 12:9. Notice, too, that Jesus binds the dragon's agents, the demons and spirits of Satan (Matthew 12:22–32; Luke

10:17–20). At the end of this 1,000-year imprisonment, the dragon is released to make war against the people of God, which again sounds like Revelation 12 when the dragon went after the offspring of the woman. What is clear is that the dragon *has been defeated in heaven* and then *has been bound by Christ*. Which means the dragon's powers now are limited. This is the first stage of the dragon's defeat and destruction, and 20:1–6 is exactly about that: the dragon's defeat.

And consider this: John writes about the "first resurrection," which pertains to the event that leads to the martyrs reigning with Christ during this so-called millennium period (20:4–6). A first resurrection is not the same as the "second" resurrection, which seems to be what happens later in this chapter when all the dead are raised for the final judgment (20:12).

So, let me put this together, however tentatively. During our present time, which is symbolized by this 1,000-year period, those who have been martyred for Christ are raised in a special way to the throne room with God to sit on thrones (20:4) and so join the twenty-four elders, who also sit on thrones (11:16), and the four living things in the presence of God. The martyrs join God and others in ruling the cosmos.

STAGE TWO

The second stage destroys the dragon (20:7–10). John's vision continues, leading him to see the dragon gathering an innumerable army that approaches Jerusalem ("the city he loves"; 20:9). The battle echoes, and seems to remix, the other battles of the dragon in Revelation (6:1–8; 9:1–21; 11:7–14; 12:13–17; 16:10–21; 19:11–21). In today's passage the dragon and all its minions are consumed by fire. Ironically, after being destroyed by fire the dragon was "thrown into the lake of burning sulfur" to join the two beasts, where they will be destroyed. Gruesome, for sure, but a fitting end for the enemies of God, justice, and peace. The prayers of the martyrs are answered (6:9–11).

DEFEATING DEATH

Death grips humans, and the dragon desires Death for all creation. With the beasts and the dragon out of the way, one last enemy still stands, death (1 Corinthians 15:26). All are summoned to stand before the "great white throne," a throne not heard of anywhere else in the Bible. The white horse rider, Faithful and True, the Word of God, our Lord Jesus, returns to eradicate evil and establish what is good. The white-throne judgment looks at the return of Christ through the lens of a final judgment. The result of both the white horse rider and the judgment are identical: the defeat and destruction of Team Dragon, and the establishment of New Jerusalem for Team Lamb.

The books are opened and the book of life is consulted. Those in the book of life enter New Jerusalem. Those who are not are "thrown into the lake of fire" with Team Dragon (20:15). Once again, apocalypse gonna apocalypse. In Jewish apocalypses fire frequently appears as the instrument for the defeat of evil and the enemies of God. Revelation 20:15, along with 14:11 and 20:10, have figured into the way some theologians envision hell. Commonly called "eternal conscious punishment" or "torment," the literalism of such a view turns what apocalyptic does well (stimulate imagination) into what it does not do at all (describe literal realities). Once again, what these verses describe is the grievous tragedies of what happens to humans who turn from God's design for them. They diminish, as C.S. Lewis once wrote in *The Great Divorce*, as weightless wraiths where the image of God seems to have diminished into barely an echo of itself.

Jesus' famous "it is finished" in John 19:30 formed the basis for Revelation 17–20's victories of Babylon, the beasts, and the dragon. With the enemies of the Lamb put to sleep, John turns to the last scene of Revelation, the new heavens and new earth and New Jerusalem (21–22).

QUESTIONS FOR REFLECTION AND APPLICATION

1. What teaching have you heard previously about the millennium? How does that compare with this interpretive approach?

2. What do you find significant about the martyrs getting to rule?

3. Read 1 Corinthians 15:26 and compare with this section. How does Revelation illustrate death as the last enemy?

4. Read Ezekiel 38–39. Mark in your Bible words and phrases and events that are echoed in Revelation 17–20.

5. How does this passage impact your understanding of hell?

FOR FURTHER READING

C.S. Lewis, *The Great Divorce* (New York: HarperOne, 2015).

A NEW CREATION
IMAGINATION

Revelation 21:1–8

¹ Then I saw "a new heaven and a new earth," for the first heaven and the first earth had passed away, and there was no longer any sea. ² I saw the Holy City, the new Jerusalem, coming down out of heaven from God, prepared as a bride beautifully dressed for her husband. ³ And I heard a loud voice from the throne saying, "Look! God's dwelling place is now among the people, and he will dwell with them. They will be his people, and God himself will be with them and be their God. ⁴ 'He will wipe every tear from their eyes. There will be no more death' or mourning or crying or pain, for the old order of things has passed away."

⁵ He who was seated on the throne said, "I am making everything new!" Then he said, "Write this down, for these words are trustworthy and true."

⁶ He said to me: "It is done. I am the Alpha and the Omega, the Beginning and the End. To the thirsty I will give water without cost from the spring of the water of life. ⁷ Those who are victorious will inherit all this, and I will be their God and they will be my children. ⁸ But the cowardly, the unbelieving, the vile, the murderers, the sexually immoral, those who practice magic arts,

the idolaters and all liars—they will be consigned to the fiery lake of burning sulfur. This is the second death."

Those who pray the Lord's Prayer's "Your kingdom come, your will be done, on earth as it is in heaven" get their prayers answered in today's passage. For the City of Justice to arrive, Babylon has to be defeated. The narrative of the Apocalypse pleads with us to let the story unfold for itself. Revelation 21–22 forms the completion of creation and the establishment of the kingdom of God to replace the corrupted systems of the dragon with its beasts and its own city, Babylon. What Revelation 21–22 reveal are more than one might expect. This is not just the defeat of Rome with all the cargo and merchants reversing course to unload at Caesarea Maritima so the stuff can all be hauled up to Jerusalem. Nor is this a Roman empire replaced by a Jerusalem empire.

No, the thematic term for these chapters is the word *NEW*, a term appearing four times in the first five verses (21:1 [twice], 2, 5). We have a *new* heaven, a *new* earth, which is the whole cosmos! We also hear of a *new* Jerusalem. To intensify the newness, the One on the Throne declares "I am making everything new!" (21:5). To make it clear that this is not up for debate, God tells John, "Write this down, for these words are [like Jesus who is the Faithful and True one (19:11)] trustworthy and true" (21:5). The NIV unfortunately translates the same word (*pistos*) in 19:11 as "faithful" but in 21:5 with "trustworthy." The word connotes the faithfulness and allegiance of God *to his promises for all creation*. When God says he is making all things new, it means all creation is becoming an all-new creation. The way a manual typewriter was radically re-created into something like but also something totally unlike it into a computer with constant upgrades until it . . . well, until it eternally becomes eternally new.

Only those with an active imagination perceive the glories of what we are about to see in these last two chapters of the Apocalypse. Only the imaginers of this world experience these visions as they are meant to be enjoyed. Nothing stimulates what is *now* like knowing what *will be*.

GOD'S CITY

John's vision is of a "new heaven and a new earth," which comes straight out of Isaiah 65:17, and *new* here means that the "first heaven and the first earth had passed away" and the embodiment of chaos and death (13:1; Daniel 7:2–3), the sea, "was no longer" (21:1). As Babylon, the beasts, and the dragon leave the stage, so also their corrupted cosmos joins them. To renew the cosmos and Babylon, John sees God lower "the Holy City, the New Jerusalem" to earth. Without helping his listeners one moment, John shifts the image from the City to the Bride (21:2), which echoes the invitation to the "wedding supper of the Lamb" (19:9). This City-Bride counters the whore of Babylon in chapter seventeen and joins hands with the woman of Revelation's twelfth chapter. She is outfitted "for her husband," who is God! (21:2). The New Jerusalem then is the people of God, as the woman of Revelation 12 was the people of God.

GOD'S THRONE-ROOM INTERPRETATION

Two voices explain what John saw. First, "a loud voice from the throne," which could make us think it is God himself but, no, this loud voice, as at 16:17 and 19:5, speaks about

God in the third person: "God's dwelling place . . . he will dwell . . . he will wipe every tear from their eyes" (21:3–4). We learn that God's City-Bride descending means (1) that God will be at home with humans by making his home with humans (21:3). God's residence among us means (2) we "will be his people and . . . God will be [our] God" (21:4). This language re-establishes and renews God's ancient covenant with Israel (Genesis 17:7–8; Jeremiah 30–32). And, (3) God will remove death, mourning, crying, and pain (Revelation 21:4). Why? Because "the old order of things has passed away."

Now the second voice, this time God's (21:5–8), which begins with "I am making everything new!" (21:5). But God explains more. First, the story of everything on earth as it was created is over. Close the book because we've read the last chapter of that story (21:6). The God who created is the God who will complete creation, and that is why God says "I am the Alpha and Omega, the Beginning and the End" (21:6; cf. 1:8; 22:13), language used both for the Father-God and for Jesus. As Creator and Completer of the cosmos, God will provide water for the thirsty and for those victors over the dragon, beasts, and Babylon, they will inherit "all this." Again, the covenant is renewed with "I will be their God and they will be my children" (21:7).

The tragedy of this God-ness of God, this glory of God, is that some humans refuse to worship God and choose Team Dragon. They will, and here John simply repeats what he has already said, "be consigned to the fiery lake" with Team Dragon. This is the "second death" (21:8).

Now to back up: God's Holy City, the New Jerusalem, the City-Bride forms a wedding-like union with God's people in a new creation world where God is eternally and covenantly related to the people and where all provisions will be available for all God's people forever and ever. A summary statement is that God will be present with God's people all together in God's place. Is that heaven? Yes, but it is not up in the sky but heaven on earth. No one fits more into this Holy City than the faithful believers of western Asia Minor.

QUESTIONS FOR REFLECTION AND APPLICATION

1. What is the importance of the word "new" in this section?

2. Why does the old have to go away before the new can come?

3. What images does John use for the people of God in his Apocalypse?

4. Which emotions does this passage stir in you?

5. What are you most looking forward to in the new creation?

HEAVEN ON EARTH

Revelation 21:9–22:5

⁹ *One of the seven angels who had the seven bowls full of the seven last plagues came and said to me, "Come, I will show you the bride, the wife of the Lamb."* ¹⁰ *And he carried me away in the Spirit to a mountain great and high, and showed me the Holy City, Jerusalem, coming down out of heaven from God.* ¹¹ *It shone with the glory of God, and its brilliance was like that of a very precious jewel, like a jasper, clear as crystal.* ¹² *It had a great, high wall with twelve gates, and with twelve angels at the gates. On the gates were written the names of the twelve tribes of Israel.* ¹³ *There were three gates on the east, three on the north, three on the south and three on the west.* ¹⁴ *The wall of the city had twelve foundations, and on them were the names of the twelve apostles of the Lamb.*

¹⁵ *The angel who talked with me had a measuring rod of gold to measure the city, its gates and its walls.* ¹⁶ *The city was laid out like a square, as long as it was wide. He measured the city with the rod and found it to be 12,000 stadia in length, and as wide and high as it is long.* ¹⁷ *The angel measured the wall using human measurement, and it was 144 cubits thick.* ¹⁸ *The wall was made of jasper, and the city of pure gold, as pure as glass.* ¹⁹ *The foundations of the city walls were decorated with every kind of precious stone. The first foundation was jasper, the second sapphire, the third agate, the fourth emerald,* ²⁰ *the fifth*

onyx, the sixth ruby, the seventh chrysolite, the eighth beryl, the ninth topaz, the tenth turquoise, the eleventh jacinth, and the twelfth amethyst. [21] The twelve gates were twelve pearls, each gate made of a single pearl. The great street of the city was of gold, as pure as transparent glass.

[22] I did not see a temple in the city, because the Lord God Almighty and the Lamb are its temple. [23] The city does not need the sun or the moon to shine on it, for the glory of God gives it light, and the Lamb is its lamp. [24] The nations will walk by its light, and the kings of the earth will bring their splendor into it. [25] On no day will its gates ever be shut, for there will be no night there. [26] The glory and honor of the nations will be brought into it. [27] Nothing impure will ever enter it, nor will anyone who does what is shameful or deceitful, but only those whose names are written in the Lamb's book of life.

[22:1] Then the angel showed me the river of the water of life, as clear as crystal, flowing from the throne of God and of the Lamb [2] down the middle of the great street of the city. On each side of the river stood the tree of life, bearing twelve crops of fruit, yielding its fruit every month. And the leaves of the tree are for the healing of the nations. [3] No longer will there be any curse. The throne of God and of the Lamb will be in the city, and his servants will serve him. [4] They will see his face, and his name will be on their foreheads. [5] There will be no more night. They will not need the light of a lamp or the light of the sun, for the Lord God will give them light. And they will reign for ever and ever.

Chicago's streets, so I'm told, were the first grid system ever built. Designed by Edward P. Brennan to counter the chaos of duplicate names and identical addresses in different parts of the city, the grid system turned chaos into the most orderly system of any major city in the USA. Here are the rules:

Remember graph paper from middle school math?
Then you can imagine the Chicago grid.
It has a north-south axis, and an east-west axis. The
center point is at State and Madison in the heart
of the Loop. That's 0 north, south, east, and west.
Each street address contains a directional prefix—N,
S, E or W.
A mile is roughly eight city blocks.*

But beware of Chicago's designed shortcut streets: diagonals radiating out from the city center. It's all very organized. If you end up in a conversation with a few Chicagoans who introduce themselves to one another, they will inevitably start describing streets and numbers. Their foreign language of this grid will amaze you, the outsider (like me). Chicago, of course, is not even close to New Jerusalem. But John's description of the Cubed Eternal City reminds me of Chicago's grid. Did you notice it was a cube?

Here are the major, mostly symbolic, features of New Jerusalem, which overall depicts an idealized, perfected society of God's people in God's new creation.

New Jerusalem Is Beautiful

One of the seven angels of the seven plagues, or bowls, summons John to come hither to see the glorious beauty of the Lamb's bride, the Body of Christ in Paul's letters, and people of God, the offspring of the woman of Revelation 12 (cf. 21:9). The Bride is the "Holy City, Jerusalem." John is taken "in the Spirit" to a mountain to spy the descent of

---

* https://news.wttw.com/2023/01/23/wttw-news-explains-how-does -chicago-s-grid-street-system-work. For more details, see https://chicago studies.uchicago.edu/grid.

the City, and what he observes is the "glory of God" and "brilliance" as of precious gems. Like a bride adorned.

In this vision John's imagery shifts from the beauty of a bride to the glory of the City itself. Once again, unlike the woman of Babylon and like the woman of Revelation 12, the beautiful city of New Jerusalem is depicted—as cities have often been—as a spectacularly beautiful woman. The most common word said, aloud or at least muttered by most of the guests, of the bride in her wedding march to "Here Comes the Bride" is "beautiful."

NEW JERUSALEM INCLUDES
ALL THE PEOPLE OF GOD

John notices for us the *twelve-ness* of this descending-to-earth City: twelve gates with twelve (guardian) angels, the names of the twelve tribes of Israel on the gates, and twelve foundations with the names of twelve apostles. Forgive anyone who wonders if the twenty-four elders are not the sum of twelve tribal leaders and twelve apostles. I would think so (4:4). The two peoples of God are not opposed to one another but complement one another. The twelve apostles continue the work of God through the twelve tribes.

NEW JERUSALEM IS A
PERFECT SHAPE

Ezekiel is the prophet behind John's remixing of prophetic images for the New Jerusalem. Only an architect loves the intense descriptions Ezekiel spied of his new Jerusalem (Ezekiel 40–48). You might just sit in a comfortable chair and read the whole sketch of Ezekiel, and you'll come away thinking *that's like and also unlike John's vision*. That's because John's is a remixing of Ezekiel's. Another vision of a new Jerusalem is found in the Dead Sea Scrolls. Again *like and unlike John's vision.*

What John sees is a perfect, massive Cubed City that outdoes Chicago's grid system. Actually, John's City is an LOL moment for unsuspecting readers: the City is 1,400 miles by 1,400 miles by 1,400 miles, and by the time he measured the City he had to be dizzy and wondering if there were some more 1,400s to measure. The City is about as large as the entire Roman empire! The City is an idealized reality, a kind of heaven on earth, and its size is big enough to hold every nation and tribe and people and language. Its walls are, get this, about 200 feet thick—wider than a football field. Not just dense, the walls are made of jasper and the City is pure gold. The twelve (apostle) foundations are made of precious stones, while each of the twelve gates (tribes of Israel) is made of one pearl. The "great street," which reflects the ancient mode of civil construction, was "of gold, as pure as transparent glass" (21:15–21).

New Jerusalem Has a No-Temple Temple

Rome was a forum. Jerusalem was a temple, the pride of the nation, if pride can be expanded to provide the chest-swelling sensations Jews felt about their temple. Josephus, a first century Jewish historian, described the beauty of the temple for his Roman readers in the following words:

> The exterior aspect of the sanctuary building made an absolutely stunning impact, both spiritual and visual. Covered all over in massive plates of gold, as soon as the sun rose it radiated such a fiery blaze of light that

anyone necessarily facing it in that direction had to avert his eyes, as if from a direct glance at the sun. To foreigners on their way to the temple it looked from the distance like a snow-clad mountain, as all not covered by the gold was pure white in color. On the roof there protruded sharp golden spikes to prevent birds perching there and fowling it. Some of the stones in the building were 68 feet long, 7.5 feet deep, and 9 feet wide. (*Jewish War* 5.222–223, translator Hammond)

One has to wonder what Jewish believers, who had always loved their temple, thought when they heard John describe New Jerusalem in which he "did not see a temple . . . because the Lord God Almighty and the Lamb are its temple" (21:22). For John, as with the author of Hebrews, the temple was a shadow of things to come (Hebrews 8:5). The reality was the presence of God and the presence of the Lamb. Once the heavenly Jerusalem descends to earth, the old temple is put aside in favor of new creation's New Jerusalem. Since God, again like Hebrews 1:1–4, was an effulgence of glory and since the Lamb was its lamp of light, neither the sun's nor the moon's light were needed.

The point of the no-temple kind of temple is exactly what Richard Lischer once said in a sermon at Duke Chapel: "I have seen the future, and it belongs to God" (Lischer, "I Have Seen the Future," 289). Amen?

New Jerusalem Includes the Nations

The New Jerusalem will be inhabited by people from the whole world. Remember these verses, 5:9; 7:9; 10:11; 14:6, which were early indications that the small band of Lamb followers would have a world-wide impact with the gospel. So we expect to hear about the nations in New Jerusalem and we are not disappointed. First, we hear a reversal of life choices when we read that the "nations will walk by its light, and the kings of the earth will bring their splendor into" the City (21:24). That the City will not need to lock up its gates at night indicates the people of this Eternal City will no longer fear the onslaughts of Babylon's armies (21:25). Instead, reversing the direction of the cargo ships, "the glory and honor of the nations" will be carried to new creation's New Jerusalem. What the nations will bring will not just be food and jewelry and spices, etc., but their cultures so that in New Jerusalem all the language will be spoken and all the cultures will be celebrated—and no ethnic group or race will be othered. Ever.

The Eternal City is for the people of God, those purified by the Lamb and who have sworn allegiance to the Lamb and who have walked in the way of the Lamb. That is those with the wisdom of the Lamb who witness to the Lamb and who worship the Lamb.

NEW JERUSALEM IS
A NEW EDEN

New Jerusalem remixes Eden with the prophets of Israel. There is a "river of the water of life," which echoes Isaiah 33:20–21 and Ezekiel 47:1–12. This river, unlike all other rivers, is "flowing from the throne of God and of the Lamb" (Revelation 22:1). Coursing straight through the City, this river of life passes by the "tree of life," which echoes Genesis 2:9–10, on each side of the street. The trees bear twelve different fruits, one per month (Revelation 22:2). That one is fun. The leaves of the tree of life "are for the healing of the nations," which again reminds us of the evangelistic impact of the gospel of the Lamb. One more echo of Eden: "No longer will there be any curse" (22:3), which echoes Genesis 3:14–19.

Two more observations: In the New Jerusalem the "servants" (NIV: the term is "slaves") of God will serve God, and what stands out is that there will be no more distance between God and humans because they "will see his face" (22:4), undoing Exodus 33:20–23, and have his name on their foreheads (Revelation 7:3; 14:1). And, as God's priestly people, they will "reign for ever and ever" (22:5).

The Bride of the Lamb, so unlike Babylon and so like the woman of Revelation 12, is the City of God, the New Jerusalem. God and the Lamb will not only dwell in this City and share an intimate relationship, but the truth of God enlightens the City for the whole world to come and share in its glories.

QUESTIONS FOR REFLECTION AND APPLICATION

1. What aspects of the description of New Jerusalem most stand out to you?

2. For Jews who cared deeply about the temple, how do you think the idea of a no-temple temple struck them?

3. Read Revelation 21:1–22:5 and list any "no more" ideas, as in no more tears and no more curse.

4. How does New Jerusalem reshape your view of heaven?

5. How does it reshape your view of life now?

FOR FURTHER READING:

Richard Lischer, "I Have Seen the Future," in *Sermons from Duke Chapel*, ed. William H. Willimon (Durham: Duke University Press, 2005), 288–292.

Scot McKnight, *The Heaven Promise: Engaging the Bible's Truth about Life to Come* (Colorado Springs: WaterBrook, 2015).

Josephus, *The Jewish War*, translated by Martin Hammond and introduction and notes by Martin Goodman (New York: Oxford University Press, 2017).

TRYING TO END
AN APOCALYPSE

Revelation 22:6–21

⁶ The angel said to me, "These words are trustworthy and true. The Lord, the God who inspires the prophets, sent his angel to show his servants the things that must soon take place."

⁷ "Look, I am coming soon! Blessed is the one who keeps the words of the prophecy written in this scroll."

⁸ I, John, am the one who heard and saw these things. And when I had heard and seen them, I fell down to worship at the feet of the angel who had been showing them to me. ⁹ But he said to me, "Don't do that! I am a fellow servant with you and with your fellow prophets and with all who keep the words of this scroll. Worship God!"

¹⁰ Then he told me, "Do not seal up the words of the prophecy of this scroll, because the time is near. ¹¹ Let the one who does wrong continue to do wrong; let the vile person continue to be vile; let the one who does right continue to do right; and let the holy person continue to be holy."

¹² "Look, I am coming soon! My reward is with me, and I will give to each person according to what they have done. ¹³ I am the Alpha and the Omega, the First and the Last, the Beginning and the End.

[14] *"Blessed are those who wash their robes, that they may have the right to the tree of life and may go through the gates into the city. [15] Outside are the dogs, those who practice magic arts, the sexually immoral, the murderers, the idolaters and everyone who loves and practices falsehood.*

[16] *"I, Jesus, have sent my angel to give you this testimony for the churches. I am the Root and the Offspring of David, and the bright Morning Star."*

[17] *The Spirit and the bride say, "Come!" And let the one who hears say, "Come!" Let the one who is thirsty come; and let the one who wishes take the free gift of the water of life.*

[18] *I warn everyone who hears the words of the prophecy of this scroll: If anyone adds anything to them, God will add to that person the plagues described in this scroll. [19] And if anyone takes words away from this scroll of prophecy, God will take away from that person any share in the tree of life and in the Holy City, which are described in this scroll.*

[20] *He who testifies to these things says, "Yes, I am coming soon."*

Amen. Come, Lord Jesus. [21] The grace of the Lord Jesus be with God's people. Amen.

John ends the Apocalypse by ending about half a dozen times. Notice how the NIV chopped up today's reading into paragraphs. Most of the paragraphs above could have ended the book but for some reason, or reasons, he kept on ending the book. Today's passage reminds me of some sermons I've heard when I thought it was over three or four times.

Except it wasn't.

Until it did end.

Gordon Fee captures my feelings about John's ending perfectly when he writes, "Nonetheless, the somewhat rambling nature of this material suggests that perhaps [John] was somewhat reluctant to let the story go" (Fee, *Revelation*, 307). Exactly. He wants to sign off but he's not quite ready to put the quill down.

John's endings of Revelation contain two themes: Foundations and Blessings and Rewards.

FOUNDATIONS

That faithfulness and truth of what John heard from the throne room and from the angels forms the first foundation. What John heard is true because "the Lord, the God who inspires the prophets, sent his angel to show his slaves [NIV: "servants"] the things that must soon take place" (22:6). John began his Apocalypse with the theme of a chain from God to John and then to the readers and listeners in western Asia Minor's seven churches (1:1–3). Add to 22:6 verse seven and ten's "prophecy" and verse sixteen and twenty's term "testimony." When it comes to the Bible's view of the Bible, pride of place must be given to Psalm 119, but a close second would be the combination of these verses in Revelation. When we add 2 Timothy 3:14–17 and 2 Peter 1:19–21 to these verses in Revelation, we have the makings of a view of the Bible: it is God's intentional spoken and written communication through Spirit and angels and humans so that the people of God will know the mind of God and, knowing the mind of God, the people of God can be and live like the people of God.

The second foundation is *imminency*, by which is meant that over and over in the New Testament, believers, because no one knows for sure, are exhorted to be continually ready for the return of Christ. In our passage we find this five times: "things that must soon take place" and "I am coming soon" and "the time is near" and "I am coming soon" and "I am coming soon" (22:6, 7, 10, 12, 20). Preparation for an any-day return of Christ stands next to the prediction that the time is "soon" or "near," which can suggest soon-ness or sudden-ness (Fee, *Revelation*, 308). God gives a prophet a vision for his or her generation, and glues just beyond that generation a vision of the final end of all history. Meaning, not only were Israel's prophets and John inspired to see the final end connected to their generation, but Jesus and Paul and James were inspired in the same way (Matthew 24:29–51; 1 Thessalonians 4:16–5:11; James 5:9). Their not-knowing is a way of exhorting us to be ready.

The third foundation is *who Jesus is*. He is the One who is coming soon (22:7, 12, 20), the judge of all (22:12), and the "Alpha and Omega, the First and the Last, the Beginning and the End" (22:13), the "Root and the Offspring of David" and the "bright Morning Star" (22:16).

The foundation for the truthfulness and faithfulness of the words of the book of Revelation, then, is formed with Jesus speaking God's words through John about his soon-return to eradicate all evil and to establish all good. Babylon, the beasts, and the dragon will lose to the Lamb's victory with the Sword-Word from the mouth of this Jesus.

BLESSINGS AND REWARDS

John repeats himself when it comes to his final words for the seven churches (and for us). We are "blessed" by God if we listen, learn, and follow the words of Jesus (22:7). And if we worship God alongside John and the revealing angels (22:8–9). And if we choose not to seal up this book by not divulging its truths to others (22:10–11). And if we live for the approving "reward" of a life well lived from Jesus (22:12–13). And we can enter into the New Jerusalem if our robes, unlike those on Team Dragon, are washed clean by Jesus (22:14–15). And if entering into New Jerusalem we "come" to receive the "water of [eternal] life" (22:17). And if we don't "add" or "subtract" words in this Apocalypse (22:18–19). Which calls for Gordon Fee one more time, who wrote, "This is apocalyptic rhetoric, of course, and has less to do with individual words as such (so that later scribes who add or omit for the sake of clarity are not thereby condemned!), and everything to do with content. Thus John concludes with a very strong sense that what he has written is indeed what he had received from Christ himself by the Spirit; and therefore these are words to be heard and thus heeded" (Fee, *Revelation*, 314).

And we are blessed with rewards from the Lord Jesus if we join with John in praying for Jesus to return (22:20).

For Team Lamb, John offers a customary prayer-wish: "The grace of the Lord Jesus be with God's people." And those who want that blessing say "Amen" (22:21).

All God's people say, "Amen!"

QUESTIONS FOR REFLECTION AND APPLICATION

1. What impact do John's multiple endings have on you as a reader?

2. What does Revelation communicate about the Bible itself?

3. Consider John's urgency and message of imminence—how might this have landed with the first hearers, and how does it land for you thousands of years later?

4. How has this study impacted your understanding of Revelation?

5. What do you want to change in your life to live more clearly on Team Lamb?

New Testament Everyday
Bible Study Series

Become a daily Bible reader attentive to the mind of God

In the New Testament Everyday Bible Study Series, each volume:
- offers brief expositions of the biblical text and offers a clear focus for the central message of each passage;
- brings the passage alive with fresh images and what it means to follow King Jesus;
- provides biblical connections and questions for reflection and application for each passage.

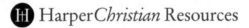

The Blue Parakeet, 2nd Edition

Rethinking How You Read the Bible

Scot McKnight, author of
The Jesus Creed

How are we to live out the Bible today? In this updated edition of *The Blue Parakeet*, you'll be challenged to see how Scripture transcends culture and time, and you'll learn how to come to God's Word with a fresh heart and mind.

The gospel is designed to be relevant in every culture, in every age, in every language. It's fully capable of this, and, as we read Scripture, we are called to discern how God is speaking to us today.

And yet applying its words and directions on how to live our lives is not as easy as it seems. As we talk to the Christians around us about issues that matter, many of us wonder: how on earth are we reading the same Bible? How is it that two of us can sit down with the same Bible and come away with two entirely different answers about everything from charismatic gifts to the ordaining of women?

Professor and author of *The King Jesus Gospel* Scot McKnight challenges us to rethink how to read the Bible, not just to puzzle it together into some systematic belief or historical tradition but to see it as an ongoing Story that we're summoned to enter and to carry forward in our day.

What we need is a fresh blowing of God's Spirit on our culture, in our day, and in our ways. We need twenty-first-century Christians living out the biblical gospel in twenty-first-century ways. And if we read the Bible properly, we will see that God never asked one generation to step back in time and live in ways of the past.

Through the Bible, God speaks in each generation, in that generation's ways and beckons us to be a part of his amazing story.

Available in stores and online!

We hope you enjoyed this Bible study from Scot McKnight.
Here are some other Bible studies we think you'll like.

N.T. Wright and
Michael F. Bird

Sandra Richter

Derwin Gray

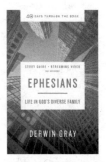

*The New Testament
You Never Knew*
Video Study

The Epic of Eden: Psalms
Video Study

*40 Days Through
the Book: Ephesians*
Video Study

Following King Jesus

We want to follow King Jesus, but do we know how?

Author and professor Scot McKnight will help you discover what it means to follow King Jesus through 24 lessons based on four of his writings (*The King Jesus Gospel, The Blue Parakeet - 2nd edition, One.Life,* and *A Fellowship of Differents*). McKnight's unique framework for discipleship is designed to be used for personal study and within disciple-making groups of two or more. In this workbook, McKnight will help you:

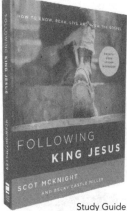

Study Guide
9780310105992

- Know the biblical meaning of the gospel
- Read the Bible and understand how to apply it today
- Live as disciples of Jesus in all areas of life
- Show the world God's character through life together in the church

Each lesson, created by Becky Castle Miller, has both Personal Study and Group Discussion sections. The Personal Study section contains a discipleship reading from Scot McKnight, an insightful Bible study, an insightful Bible study, and a time for individual prayer, action, and reflection. The Group Discussion section includes discussion questions and activities to do together with a discipleship group. You'll share insights from your personal study time with each other and explore different ways of living out what you're learning.

Whether you have been a Christian for many years or you are desiring a fresh look at what it means to be a disciple, this workbook is an in-depth guide to what it means to follow King Jesus and to discover how to put that kind of life into practice.

 Harper*Christian*
Resources